PAINTBOX ON THE FRONTIER

The Life and Times of George Caleb Bingham

PAINTBOX ON THE FRONTIER

The Life and Times of George Caleb Bingham

Illustrated with Reproductions

BY ALBERTA WILSON CONSTANT

Thomas Y. Crowell Company   *New York*

Copyright © 1974 by Alberta Wilson Constant

All rights reserved. Except for use in a review, the reproduction or utilization of this work in any form or by any electronic, mechanical, or other means, now known or hereafter invented, including xerography, photocopying, and recording, and in any information storage and retrieval system is forbidden without the written permission of the publisher. Published simultaneously in Canada by Fitzhenry & Whiteside Limited, Toronto.

Designed by Sallie Baldwin

Manufactured in the United States of America

1   2   3   4   5   6   7   8   9   10

Library of Congress Cataloging in Publication Data
Constant, Alberta Wilson.
    Paintbox on the frontier.
    1.   Bingham, George Caleb, 1811-1879.   I.   Title.
ND237.B59C66   759.13   73-6954
ISBN 0-690-60844-6

Acknowledgments

Acknowledgement is gratefully made for permission to quote from the following copyrighted material:

From *George Caleb Bingham: The Evolution of an Artist* by E. Maurice Bloch. Originally published by the University of California Press. Copyright © 1967. Reprinted by permission of The Regents of the University of California.

From *Gray Ghosts of the Confederacy: Guerilla Warfare in the West, 1861-1865* by Richard S. Brownlee. By permission of the publisher Louisiana State University, copyright © 1958.

From *George Caleb Bingham of Missouri* by Albert Christ-Janer. By permission of the publisher Dodd, Mead & Company, copyright © 1940.

From *George Caleb Bingham: River Portraitist* by John Francis McDermott. Courtesy of Mercantile Library, St. Louis. Copyright © 1959 by the University of Oklahoma Press.

From *The Heritage of Missouri—A History* by Duane Meyer, State Publishing Co., rev. ed., 2nd printing. Copyright © 1963. By permission of the author.

From *The Missouri* by Stanley Vestal. By permission of the publisher, the University of Nebraska Press. Copyright © 1945 by Walter Stanley Campbell. Bison Book edition reprinted from the 1945 edition, third printing, by arrangement with Holt, Rinehart & Winston, Inc.

The author is also grateful to the State Historical Society of Missouri and the *Missouri Historical Review* for permission to quote from:

C. B. Rollins, "Some Recollections of George Caleb Bingham." *Missouri Historical Review*, XX, No. 1 (Oct. 1926-July 1926).

C. B. Rollins, ed., "Letters of George Caleb Bingham to James S. Rollins," *Missouri Historical Review* XXXII Nos. 1-4 (Oct., 1937-July 1938); Ibid. XXXIII Nos. 1-4 (Oct., 1938-July 1939).

Marie George Windell, "The Road West in 1818, The Diary of Henry Vest Bingham," *Missouri Historical Review*, XL, Nos. 1-2 (Oct. 1945-Jan. 1946).

William G. Bek, trans., Paul Wilhelm, Duke of Wuerttemberg, *First Journey to North America in the Years 1822-1824* (Stuttgart & Tuebingen, Germany, 1855). Typescript in the State Historical Society of Missouri.

From "George Caleb Bingham: The Artist as Social Historian" by John Demos, *American Quarterly*, Vol. XVII No. 2, Part 1, Summer 1965. Copyright, 1965, Trustees of University of Pennsylvania.

From "The Nelson Gallery Acquires a Long Lost Bingham Painting" by Winifred Shields, Kansas City *Star*, October 31, 1954.

Quotations from early Missouri newspapers come from the Newspaper Library of the State Historical Society of Missouri or from the collection in the Missouri Valley Room of the Kansas City Public Library.

Letters quoted, unless otherwise stated, come from the Bingham Family Papers, 1814-1930, in the State Historical Society of Missouri.

By the Author

MISS CHARITY COMES TO STAY
THE MOTORING MILLERS
PAINTBOX ON THE FRONTIER: *The Life and Times of
George Caleb Bingham*
THOSE MILLER GIRLS!
WILLIE AND THE WILDCAT WELL

This book is lovingly dedicated to
the memory of Jonathan Abebe Ewing

In Appreciation

Many people helped me write this story of George Caleb Bingham and his times. I remember their generosity with their time and effort; I remember their patience. No list could be made that would include every name. But I can say "thank you," and I can hope that those who helped me and who now read the book will in some measure be pleased.

Dozens of owners of Bingham paintings let me come into their homes to see their treasures. Since some of them asked not to be identified, it seems best to thank them in this way. They were a kind and thoughtful group of people, deeply appreciative of the work of the artist.

Mrs. Clara King Bowdry, Bingham's granddaughter, and Mrs. Clara B. Whittington, his great-granddaughter, helped me with family recollections, information, and best of all, encouragement. I am grateful to them.

To Ross Taggart, Senior Curator of the William Rockhill Nelson Gallery of Art, goes my heartfelt thanks for many things, but especially for allowing me to use the fine collection of slides of Bingham's work owned by the gallery.

The libraries and historical societies where I worked gave me complete cooperation. The following list has only a few individual names, but there were many others. To each of them, my thanks.

Mid-Continent Public Library (Independence, Mo.), Miss Ethel Tiffy, Miss Margaret McMillan.

Kansas City Public Library, Missouri Valley Room, Miss Marge Kinney, Mrs. Peggy Smith.

University of Missouri at Kansas City Library, Mrs. Helen Bennett.

Mercantile Library Association, St. Louis, Mrs. Elizabeth Kirchner, Miss Mary Mewes.

Jackson County (Mo.) Historical Society Archives, Mrs. Mayme Piper, Mrs. Pauline Fowler.

Kansas City Museum of History and Science, Mrs. Maxine Schell.

State Historical Society of Missouri, Dr. Richard S. Brownlee and his
entire staff.
Missouri Historical Society, St. Louis.
Library of the Pennsylvania Academy of Fine Arts, Philadelphia.
Library of the Metropolitan Museum of Art, New York.
Library of the Cincinnati Museum of Art, Cincinnati, Ohio.

Three gentlemen, authors of books about Bingham—Professor John Francis McDermott, Dr. E. Maurice Bloch, and Lew Larkin of the Kansas City *Star*—were extremely generous with information and encouragement. My special thanks also go to W. Howard Adams of the Administrative Staff of the National Gallery of Art; Dr. Philip C. Brooks, former Director of the Truman Library; Philip C. Brooks, Jr., of the National Achives, and Mrs. Ruth Rollins Westfall of Columbia, Missouri; Robert Tindall, artist, of Independence, Missouri; Mrs. C. W. Cleverdon, Lexington, Missouri; and the late Lon G. Amick of William Jewell College, Liberty, Missouri; each made a special contribution to my research.

To my friends at Thomas Y. Crowell Company and to Miss Marilyn Marlow, all of New York City, my appreciation of their patience. It has been a long four years!

Last, most, and always to my husband, Edwin B. Constant, who drove hundreds of miles, searched newspaper files, read microfilm when my eyes gave out, and otherwise endured the special problems of living with a writer working on a book—thank you.

Contents

Illustrations

COLOR PLATES

Sketch No. 74
Courtesy, St. Louis Mercantile Library

Virginia Childhood

George Caleb Bingham, who was to be known as "the Missouri artist," was not born in Missouri, but in Augusta County, Virginia. There in the beautiful Shenandoah Valley, west of the Blue Ridge Mountains, he lived on a family plantation of more than a thousand acres. His father, Henry Vest Bingham, raised tobacco on the land. His mother, Mary, was the only child of Matthias Amend, a miller of German descent, who operated a gristmill and sawmill powered by the water of South River.

The land had originally belonged to Matthias Amend, but when his daughter married, he gave it all to her and her husband. He asked only that he have a home with them for the rest of his life. George was born on this plantation, March 20, 1811. As a child he had dark-brown curly hair and dark eyes that sparkled. There is no picture to show it but the strongly marked jawline ending in a cleft chin that characterized his appearance in later life was probably there when he was a boy. Members of his father's family seeing him undoubtedly smiled, nodded, and said, "There's the Bingham stubbornness, plain as day."

The Binghams already had one son, two years older than George. He was a husky red-haired boy named Matthias after his grandfather. Two boys so near in age can have a fine time together, growing up on a plantation. Add to this the mill with a millrace, a millpond, and great turning wheels, and there can hardly be a better place. The mill wheels, George said, were the earliest things he remembered. His grandfather, Matthias Amend, had built those wheels, for he was a millwright as well as a miller.

Up-and-over-and-down, up-and-over-and-down, the water turned the wheels. The big grinding stones went around and around. Brown wheat became white flour; yellow corn became golden cornmeal. When a load of pine trees was brought down from the Blue Ridge, the flashing saws ripped them into strips of lumber. The smell of resin from the pine and the warm sweetish smell of grinding grain mingled in the air. Piles of sawdust grew into mountains to be climbed up and rolled down. Wheat in the whole grain chewed by strong young teeth makes a fine mouthful, like latter-day chewing gum. Chips tossed into the millrace bob up again as the foaming water pours into the smooth millpond. Such things were a part of George's childhood.

A mill in the early nineteenth century was much more than a place of business. It was a gathering place, where news was heard and passed along. The miller's rate was "pay a bushel to grind a bushel," so the farmers had to haul twice the amount of grain they needed to take home enough for their families and their livestock. This meant heavy loads. Oxen were better for such loads than horses. When the slow-moving ox teams reached the mill, the farmer had to wait his turn, and often he must camp by the mill for a few days. Sometimes a farmer would bring along his family for the trip, and in this way George and Matthias got acquainted with many more people than was usual for plantation children.

The nearest large town on the other side of the mountains was Charlottesville; Mr. Jefferson lived close to it at his home, Monticello. The American Revolution was a living memory in George's time. The British colonel Banastre Tarleton had terrorized the countryside. Men who had fought with George Washington were still alive for a small boy to look at and listen to. The deep devotion George felt for his country, and to the ideal of *Union,* had its roots in these years.

Nearer than Charlottesville by eighteen miles was another tobacco plantation owned by George's other grandfather. His name, also, was George Bingham. To this, in admiration for Virginia's great general, he had added the middle name of Washington. In addition to raising tobacco, George Washington Bingham was a local Methodist preacher. This means that he preached to a congregation of his neighbors, his slaves, and their slaves in the small chapel that he had built on his land.

George said of this grandfather: "I remember him well as a tall white-headed old gentleman, overflowing with the milk of human kindness." Although George Washington Bingham owned slaves, as was the custom of the times, George recalled him as being "exceedingly kind and indulgent [to them], never using the lash or allowing it to be used on his place."

No regular school broke into the easy-going life enjoyed by George and Matthias. They had lessons at home. Mary Bingham taught her children as she had once taught her father. Matthias Amend, born in York County, Pennsylvania, could not read or write English. Determined that Mary be educated, he had sent her to a boarding school, six miles from the mill. Each Friday when she came home, she went over with him all that she had learned during the week. On Sunday evening she returned to boarding school. In this way her father learned to read, to write, and to figure, and Mary learned to teach. It was a skill that she loved. When her own children came along, it was only natural that she should be their teacher.

George was about four years old when his father picked up the boy's slate one day and drew a figure on it. Exactly what figure is not known, but it was some object that was foreshortened, using a kind of simple perspective. It may have been a box or a slant-roofed house. To Henry's astonishment George took the slate and drew the same figure. Pleased, Henry drew more figures, and little George copied each one.

Did Mary stop to watch, pleased by the pleasure of her family? Perhaps Elizabeth who was barely three may have been entertained by watching her father and brother. Soon enough it was time for supper, and the pictures were washed from the slate. It was a very long time before any of the grown-ups remembered this slight incident.

But the pleasure of drawing pictures was not erased from George's mind as quickly as the pictures were erased from the slate. He liked to draw, and he kept at it. He began finding more and bigger surfaces to draw pictures on—the side of the barn, the pumphouse, the smokehouse. Wherever he found a smooth space, he drew.

A good farmer prides himself on the neatness of his farm

buildings. Henry Bingham was a very good farmer. It must have tried his patience to come upon George's scrawlings of dogs, pigs, cows, cats, flowers, trees, or whatever on the buildings. But the boy was not reprimanded. Possibly Henry sighed and thought that whitewash was cheap, and when the buildings were next whitewashed, the pictures could be covered over. Anyway the pictures stayed. With five children—Matthias, George, Elizabeth, Isaac Newton, and Henry Vest, Jr.—a man has no time to be picky about every little thing.

Henry had other things on his mind. Money was hard to get; interest rates were high. A tobacco crop was subject to the ups and downs of the market, the weather, and all the other uncertainties that plague a farmer. He was also enlarging the gristmill.

At some time during this troubled period a neighbor asked Henry to sign a note with him. The Bingham land was put up as security for the loan. What happened to the neighbor is not known, but Henry Bingham lost his land "through a security debt."

In 1818 George was seven years old. He would not have been told about the knotty financial problem his family faced. Matthias at nine would have known little more. But both boys must have sensed, as children do, the worries of their parents.

This was a painful time for Henry. He had never faced failure before. He was a big man, six feet tall, weighing over a hundred and eighty pounds. The operation of 1180 acres of land, plus the mills, called for careful management and special skills. These he had always provided. He had taken good care of his family. What was he to do now?

The tallow dips burned late as he sat, figured, frowned, and figured again. Another baby was expected. That would bring the number of children to six. And there was Matthias Amend. Nine people's lives depended on the decisions Henry would make.

As men brought grain to the mill and waited their turn at the grinding, Henry heard talk of new land—cheap land, rich land. In the West this land was waiting. The government was encouraging settlers to come into Ohio, Indiana, Illinois, and Missouri to take up land.

At the little chapel where his father preached, when Henry gathered with the neighbors for the visiting that was a big part of the service, there was more and more talk of going West. At the taverns, at the blacksmith shop, he heard of one family after another pulling up roots and leaving Virginia for the West. Henry Bingham decided that this was the best course of action.

For a man to make such a decision took courage. The cheap rich land was also wild and unsettled. Trouble with the Indians was possible. Henry and Mary were Virginia-born and -bred. Neither had ever been outside of the Old Dominion. What about the children? Matthias was stout enough, but young George had more than his share of childish ailments. The others were so little they would need years of care. Could he provide for them on the frontier? How was a man to know?

Henry kept on asking questions of those who stopped at the mill. Their information about the West was as sketchy as his. As time went on, he saw, as did many others, that if he wanted to know more about the West he would have to go there to find out for himself.

So a group of friends, neighbors, and kinsfolk banded together with one common purpose—a scouting expedition to the West. If the land was as good as they had been told, they would move there. Some planned to move together, to settle on adjoining tracts. Others, more cautious—and Henry was one of these—wanted to look over the prospects before making the final break.

In the early summer of 1818, as the sun burned through the haze of the Blue Ridge, Henry said good-bye to his family and joined a party of Virginians bound for the West. It was a solemn time. Some men who had gone West had never returned. There was danger, not only from Indians, but from the very land itself—the rivers, the forests, the trackless prairies.

An old Scottish ballad, common in the Blue Ridge, describes the thoughts of the families left behind as their men rode away:

High upon Highlands,
And low upon Tay,
Bonnie George Campbell
Rode out one day.

Saddled and bridled,
Gallant rode he,
Home came his good horse,
But never came he . . . .

Watching and waving, the Binghams stood as the tall man on horseback rode through the gate to join the others. He waved back, his gloved hand holding his hat to make the wave a little higher. His saddlebags were well filled; a blanket rolled in oilskins was snug behind the saddle; his flintlock rifle, loaded but not primed, was in easy reach.

Tom, one of the black men who worked at the mill, was by the gate waiting for Henry's last instructions. They talked for a moment. There was the soft clatter of horses' hoofs muffled by the dust, then the creak of the following wagons. The scouting expedition was moving out.

"Good-bye . . . Good-bye . . . Take care . . . Good-bye. . . ."

The shouts met, mingled, and then dropped into that curious final silence that follows the word good-bye. Dust rose from the road, and the morning sun caught the particles and turned them into a bright cloud that lingered after the wagons and horses had carried the party around the bend in the road, out of sight.

After the excitement of seeing Henry off, life settled down to its regular rhythm. Summer on a plantation was such a busy time that there was hardly space in it to worry about an absent member of the family. George, like all seven-going-on-eight-year-olds, had his own projects.

One was trying to find colors to add to his pictures. Axle grease from the mill was a good dependable black, easy to come by, but he longed for colors. He tried his mother's dye pots. In the nineteenth century, cloth was spun, dyed, and woven at home. There was butternut for brown, indigo for blue, and madder for red. Onion skins made a yellow, and a passable pink came from sumac berries. These, however, worked much better on the yarns his mother prepared for weaving than they did on the wood and stone surfaces George used for his pictures. So he learned early that color is not the same on different surfaces.

Around the yard were scattered some of the soft old hand-baked bricks left over from when the house was built. Broken into "brickbats," these could be rubbed together to make a reddish-brown dust. By mixing the dust with oil from the kitchen, George found a "paint" that would stick on a wall. There is a family story that he even "clipped the ends of his fingers" to get blood to use as red paint. A youngster as bright as George would discover quickly that blood does not keep its fine red color for long. After a trial or so, he probably went on to some less painful experiment.

Henry's absence that summer meant more work and more responsibility for Mary Bingham. With another baby coming in November and the management of the plantation on her shoulders, it is doubtful if there were many lessons. George and Matthias may have taken this chance to explore the famous Wier's Cave on the Bingham land. Swimming in the millpond was great for hot weather. Fishing for bream, picking apples, watching the haying with the rabbits scampering ahead of the scythe, all came along in due season.

Elizabeth, Isaac Newton, and Henry, Jr., the baby, had all the time in the world to play. Red corncobs from the mill could be used to build a playhouse. A small stick with a hollyhock-blossom skirt was a play lady for the house. Striped butterbeans strung in a necklace made fine jewelry for Elizabeth. They may have had tea parties with acorn cups, using watered molasses for tea. Elizabeth as the only girl could borrow her mother's thimble to cut out tiny cookies and "thimble biscuit" to be baked in the house. George may have taken part in some of these games, though like most older brothers he felt vastly superior to the little ones.

If any letter came from Henry, it has not survived the years. Mail was rare and expensive. Six cents paid for a letter going 30 miles, twenty-five cents for one going 450 miles. The Virginia party crossed the state following "stage and post roads," so some mail routes had been established. When any letter came back, it would be shared by the families of the Shenandoah Valley who had members in the scouting expedition.

At the very western tip of Virginia the party crossed over into Tennessee by the Cumberland Gap. This was the trail Daniel Boone had blazed, and the road was called by his name. They followed the Boone Trail across the mountains and up into Kentucky. There they stopped at Colonel Boone's establishment, Boonsborough. Daniel and his sons had already moved on to Missouri.

Boonsborough in 1818 was "a thinly inhabited place, the buildings fast going to rack." This was the description that Henry Vest Bingham wrote in his *Diary* of the trip. He was careful about keeping it. In it he entered the kind of land they had passed that day, the price per acre, the crops produced, the nearby streams, the conditions of the roads—all the things a man would need to know if he wanted to settle down and make a living in the area.

But the *Diary* was not wholly devoted to facts and figures. Henry described the people he met, the Indians he saw, the taverns and inns where the party stopped. Anyone who reads his *Diary,* written more than a hundred and fifty years ago, will get a good idea of the country Henry saw. He had an eye for color. As he writes about everyday happenings, they become clear to the reader. His spelling may be a bit different from ours, or even from the accepted standards of his time, but his *Diary* is lively, interesting from first to last. He was a careful observer.

Did Henry pass along this trait of careful observation to his son George? If so, was it by training? Or did the boy pick it up in unconscious imitation of the father he loved? Years later, George was to paint the world that Henry described, the Western frontier, as few artists have been able to do. And as none can do now, for that world no longer exists.

On went the scouting expedition, through Kentucky and into Indiana. Their numbers were fewer now. Some families had found land they liked. Neighbor took up land beside neighbor, transporting a small section of the Old Dominion to the new West.

Henry was not yet ready to settle. He looked carefully at Indiana: "Sulpher Spring [is] at French Lick where we could smell the Sulpher by the time we were within a half mile of the Springs . . . [the water] tasted like the washings of a Dirty Gun. . . . no doubt but Vincennes will soon be a place of Considerable Importance . . . the handsomest town in the United States."

Guidebooks were published for these westward-moving parties. They described the inns on the route as "liberal, often sumptuous." This was entirely different from the true state of things, as Henry discovered. Inns along the better-traveled roads were spaced about a day's journey apart. Henry described one in his *Diary*. It was a one-room house with two small beds. Ten men wanted sleeping space. Four got the beds, and the rest were put on pallets on the floor. "Our Little Land Lady having no other place to retreat to verry nimbly crept under the bed where she staid till morning."

The food was coarse and miserably cooked. Bedbugs turned the nights into nightmares. Horseflies came in swarms during the day. These bloodsucking flies could drive a team of horses into bolting, running away to escape. Some wagons traveled at night to avoid the horseflies. A woman whose name is lost to history wrote to President Monroe from early Ohio: "Your patience sir will not hold out while I would describe the swarms of large flies which inhabit these uncultivated lands and which stinging the cattle nearly drive them to madness."

The roads, Henry wrote, "are altogether in a state of nature, trees only just chopped off a foot above the ground, stones, rocks, gullies, left to be got over as best we can; no wonder that you see a blacksmith's shop every 2–3 miles, and a tavern by the side of it to put up and spend yr money while repairs are doing."

But nowhere in his *Diary* is a hint that Henry considered turning back. Americans had a saying about the westward pioneers, "The cowards never started, and the weaklings died on the way." Henry was neither a coward nor a weakling. He was a man who had made up his mind that the best chance for him and his family lay in the West. He had set his face in that direction, and that was that. Henry, too, had his full share of "the Bingham stubbornness."

The fertility of the land they saw, untouched as yet by the

plow, was a marvel to the western emigrants. They blessed the foresight of their fellow Virginian, Thomas Jefferson, for having made the Louisiana Purchase only fifteen years before. Pioneers of those times always first chose land that was heavily timbered, believing that a treeless plain was not fertile. Besides, they needed timber for houses. So Henry listed some of the trees they were passing, "instead of white oake, black oake, wallnut, ash, wild cherry, Sugar Tree." He even noticed the weeds that grew tall and thick, "wild Cumphry . . . May Apple. . . ."

As they journeyed on, Henry began to have second thoughts about farming. He saw the great numbers of families with their household goods packed into wagons jolting past. The group of Virginians was small compared to the hundreds of travelers.

If all these people were moving West, then it stood to reason that they were going to require many services. With half an eye a man could see the demand for bricklayers, blacksmiths, coopers, stonecutters, gunsmiths, for all manner of skilled trades. There must be ropewalks for spinning rope, sawmills to cut and shape the lumber into houses, warehouses to hold the bales of furs coming down the great rivers. And there must be taverns, *good* taverns. Henry shuddered and felt his stomach turn as he thought of some of the places he had stayed in on the road. Good taverns were needed by all means!

So far the Indians he had seen looked peaceable enough. In the *Diary* he described the Kaskaskia Indians in their bright garments: "Red and Blue Leggens and Mogasons. Some handsomely worked with pockerpine quills." The women of the tribe, he noted, rode astride their horses, like the men.

After Vincennes the next goal of the party was St. Louis. At the Land Office there they hoped to get reliable information about good places for settlement. The travel-battered wagons could be repaired; the weary men and women take some rest. They could buy some provisions and even enjoy some of the pleasures brought by the French settlers to the city. In St. Louis, a history of that day says, "Not all children were taught to read, but all were taught to dance. After Mass each Sunday a ball was held somewhere in town."

Timothy Flint, another traveler of those days, wrote of "the praira" near St. Louis. "In the time of strawberries thousands of acres are reddened with the finest quality of this delicious fruit." What a treat for men and women who had lived for weeks on johnnycake and salt bacon!

As summer ended and fall came on, the Bingham family in Virginia began to expect Henry's return. The weather cooled. George was kept indoors much of the time, for he took cold easily. These were the days for books.

Both Henry and Mary owned books. Mary had bought books in her boarding-school days and added to them by purchases from itinerant book peddlers. Henry's education, George later said, "was only such as could be acquired in the common field schools of the time, but he was a constant reader. . . ." Put together these books made up a good small library. Many of them had steel engravings for illustrations, for that was then the fashion. A boy who made his own pictures would turn the pages until he found pictures made by others. His bright dark eyes would fix on the pictures. . . . The pictures . . . How were they made? He would stare a long time until he turned the page and found another.

George's own pictures were still on the farm buildings. Wrapped against the chilly wind, he snatched quick looks at them as he ran back and forth on one errand or another. Indoors was his slate for more drawing. A slate keeps no record of pictures drawn. A mistake? Whish! and it's gone. Another picture and another. There is magic in a slate.

Days passed, and now it was time for coon hunting. At night George heard the hounds as they chased their quarry up hill and down dale. Soon he and Matthias would be old enough to go along with the hunters. But would they be there to go? Would there be coons and hounds in Missouri?

Where was Missouri anyway? And above all, why didn't his father come home?

2

Sketch No. 2
Courtesy, St. Louis Mercantile Library

The Move to Missouri

Frost touched the Blue Ridge with its special glory. The trees were red and gold and brown. Dark green pines made a background for the rioting colors of the maples, the oaks, and the sycamores. On one of those days when the leaves were a Joseph's coat of many colors, Henry Bingham rode home from the West.

His clothes were weather-stained; his boots were scarred; his saddlebags were limp and flat. But there was excitement and happiness in his voice and bearing. To use the old frontier words, "He had seen the elephant!"

Henry had ridden back by way of Nashville and Shawnee-town. Even an attack of "Bold Hives" had not slowed him down. He had found what he wanted, and now he planned to go back and take his family with him. George's eyes grew big with wonder as he listened to his traveler father's tales.

Over and over he heard Henry declare that the Missouri country was the finest land in the world. His father was not alone in thinking this. Wilson Smith, another Virginia emigrant wrote, "I never saw such corn in my life . . . we will have to take ladders to climb up to the ears." Augustus Storrs, a French merchant, wrote about "the great quantities of grapes." One unknown frontier wit stated, "The land is so rich you may plant crowbars at night, and it will sprout ten-penny nails by morning."

Henry had only traveled as far as St. Charles, a little more than twenty miles from St. Louis. Why did he feel so strongly about the Missouri Territory that stretched for miles and miles, beyond the known boundaries, to the West?

The answer is that he had listened to the enthusiastic reports of other men who had gone farther. He saw the crowds bound for the interior of the territory. And he had a very important source of reliable firsthand information in Governor William Clark.

Clark, a fellow Virginian, was younger brother to George Rogers Clark, the American Revolutionary leader in the Northwest Territory. Henry would have already known him by reputation. William Clark had been sent with Meriwether Lewis by President Jefferson on the famous Lewis and Clark Expedition, which had discovered the headwaters of the Missouri River and then gone on westward to the Pacific Ocean. "The Corps of Discovery" had returned in triumph to St. Louis in September 1806. Seven years later, Clark had been appointed governor of the Territory of Missouri by James Madison. All these well-known Virginia names sounded reassuring to Mary and to Matthias Amend as Henry talked.

Governor Clark had made Henry and his party welcome. He had become Henry's host, offered him his official rooms for writing, and let Henry use his maps for locating land.

George and Matthias pressed closer to their father as he described the warmth of the governor's reception. It was something special to be a son of Henry Bingham! George pushed his dark curly hair back from his eyes and took pleasure in being reassured that he "favored his father's side of the family." Matthias had the satisfaction of learning that Governor Clark also had red hair. Clark's Indian friends, and he had many of them, called him "Red Head."

When Henry finished telling his family all that he had been able to find out about the new country, he did not have to tell them his decision. He was going back, and they were going with him. In all the Territory of Missouri, Henry had decided that the area known as the Boon's Lick country was the best place to settle. And in the Boon's Lick, the best place was the town of Franklin.

Now the rhythm of the plantation and the mill shifted. Everything had to be thought of in regard to the coming move. As the big mill wheels turned, Matthias Amend began to set aside the best meal and flour for the journey. Shelled corn and oats for the livestock, small grain for the poultry, must be carried along. The finest smoked meat was left in the smokehouse for the day of departure.

Anyone who has moved from one house to another knows the upset that it brings to a family. To move across the country to a town that none of them—not even Henry—had ever seen was much harder. The journey would be made in wagons, and they must carry along everything that would be needed on the road, as well as what would be needed on the frontier when they came to Franklin.

Every object in the house had to be considered. Should it be taken? Should it be left behind? The bulk of the decisions rested on Mary Bingham. She went about her tasks quietly, mindful of the needs of her family, and of the child she was carrying.

If George felt any anxiety at being uprooted from his Virginia home, he never mentioned it later. This speaks well for the secure feeling within the Bingham family. They were going, but they were going *together;* George and the other children probably thought of the whole thing as a big adventure—and it was.

On the fourth of November 1818, the work of getting ready to move came to a halt. On that day Frances Louisa Bingham was born. This changed the family order: Henry, Jr., was no longer "the baby"; Elizabeth was no longer the only girl. As for George, he moved a bit further up the line as next-to-oldest. In March, George would be eight years old, and Matthias ten.

The Binghams of Augusta County were a large family. Henry had seven brothers and sisters, many nieces and nephews. As these kinsfolk came to see the new baby and to say good-bye to the family, Henry told them of the glories of the new country and of the trip he had taken. George heard the tales over and over. Some of them were Indian stories.

This was an uneasy subject. Many tales circulated about white children stolen and kept captive by the Indians. Listening, George may have felt some qualms. Henry told of seeing in the streets of St. Louis breech-clouted, moccasined Sioux, trailing buffalo robes from their shoulders. He wrote about them in his *Diary:* "With Square well-proportioned faces and a Serious countenance which would seem to Bespeak a Strong Mind if cultivated . . . upon the whole I have never seen 100 men in my life so stout looking as was 100 of them that passed through the street this afternoon."

It is doubtful that George had ever in his life seen a hundred men together. To think about a hundred Indians was scary. He cannot be blamed if he worried a little.

Now the winter was gone, and spring had come in. All the choices as to what to take and what to leave behind had been made. Frances Louisa was a healthy baby, well able to travel. Two wagons had been bought to carry the family and their possessions. The supplies for the journey and the household goods were ready. They waited only for the roads to dry. Henry had seen mud that was wagon-bed deep in Indiana and Illinois. The sight had made him cautious.

No inventory of the Binghams' possessions exists, but there are accounts of other families who made the same kind of journey. The Arnold family who moved from Virginia to Lafayette County, Missouri, took "flocks and herds of cows and horses . . . [they] rode at a leisurely pace set by the cows. . . . The Negroes walked, milked the cows morning and night. Each Negro had at least ten dogs." The Oldham family came from Kentucky to Missouri, "with all their possessions, cows, horses, farm implements. . . . there were enough children, white and black, and family dogs, to make the time and distance short. My mother said they ran, walked, and played much of the way from Mt. Sterling, Kentucky, to Independence, Missouri, riding only when there were good stretches of road when the horses could go fast."

There is no suggestion that the Binghams took their slaves with them on the trip to Missouri, and no mention of them later. They must have been left behind with the new owners of the Virginia property. Some cows to provide milk for the children and some horses for riding and for pulling the wagons were a necessity. Barrels of flour and cornmeal made good ballast in the bottoms of the wagons. A keg of molasses for "long sweet-ening" was hoisted in. Hams and sides of bacon rode in the top layer.

Mary would be unlike other Virginia mothers unless she brought along some flowers dug from her garden. A favorite shrub or two was certainly there—a smoke tree or a lavender bush. The scent of lemon verbena leaves helped keep the air fresh under the wagon covers. A pouch of tobacco seed, very fine and very expensive, was carried by Henry. The family Bible was carefully packed, and so was the little library of books, impor-tant to George.

At last the great day came. The little caravan set off.

"The journey that lay ahead was immense and terrible," wrote William Cobbett, the British journalist and reformer. "The rugged roads, the dirty hovels, the fire in the woods to sleep by, the pathless ways through the wilderness, the danger-ous crossing of the rivers."

Cobbett was right. The journey was all of those things, but it was other things, too. It was adventure, and it was hope. Thomas Jefferson recognized those qualities when he wrote a friend that he never knew a person who had left the coast for land in the West to then return to the seaboard.

George Caleb Bingham, a boy of eight, was going to a new world. Behind him were the pictures he had scrawled wherever he could. Ahead of him—far, far ahead—were the pictures he would paint of the new world he was entering.

Henry had to go much slower on this his third trip over-land between Virginia and Missouri. A man on horseback can go many places that a man with a family of nine, two loaded wagons, and assorted cows, horses, dogs, and poultry would hesi-tate to go. If he "let the cows set the pace," as the Arnold family had done, then the trip went at a slow pace. Anyone who has tried to drive cows knows that they are contrary, stubborn, slow-moving creatures. George and Matthias were the right age to be "cow boys." It would be up to them to watch for strays, take the cows to water, and herd them along in their deliberate way.

What else would boys do on a journey like this? Go fishing in the many clear little streams that edged the roads and come in with pan fish for supper. Their grandfather liked to fish, too, and he may have gone off with them and passed along an old fisherman's wisdom to his grandsons. A yarn ball tossed back and forth over the slow-moving wagons makes a good game for good weather. A pocketknife gives a whittler a handy way to pass the time. A slingshot, a bean shooter, tucked into a shirt pocket can be used on unlimited targets.

The books were safely packed away for the trip, but Mary, the good teacher, may have given out spelling words around the campfire. Geography in daily lessons at home was something in a book. Here it was part of their life. Simple sums in arithmetic about the miles traveled, or the feed needed for the livestock, were provided by the very journey itself.

In those days everybody sang. There were old ballads, hymn tunes, play-party songs—all kinds of music. The wagon wheels turned a little faster to the tune of "Weev'ly Wheat," a song any miller's family would know.

> It's step her to your weev'ly wheat,
> It's step her to your barley.
> It's step her to your weev'ly wheat,
> To bake a cake for Charley.
>
> The higher up the cherry tree,
> The riper grow the cherries.
> The more you hug and kiss the girls,
> The sooner you will marry.

The verses go on and on, and even the smallest child could join in by clapping hands. The older children would teach the younger ones a drop-the-handkerchief game with,

> I-tisket, I-tasket, a green and yellow basket,
> I took a letter to my love,
> And on the way I dropped it. . . .

And when the sad ballad of "Barbara Allen" was sung, there would be tears for the unfortunate lovers. And always there were hymns to sing, reminding the travelers in the deep forest of God's love and care. The pioneers carried songs with them as they carried seed for crops or cattle for new herds.

Henry took his family over the first route that he and the scouting expedition had traveled—the Boone Trail. Did they make it to "the praira" near St. Louis in the time of strawberries? If not, there were other wild fruits—pawpaws, blackberries, chokecherries, and the tiny hackberries that birds and children love.

A ferry across the Mississippi River at St. Louis had existed since 1797. In the year that the Binghams made the crossing, it had been bought by Samuel Wiggins. He began the use of horse-tread ferries, and named his three ferryboats the *Sea Serpent,* the *Rhinoceros,* and the *Antelope.*

One of these took the Binghams and their wagons to the west bank of the river, so that they could enter St. Louis. This was the first real city George had ever seen.

In 1819, St. Louis was still very much a French city. Henry in his trip the year before had noted in his *Diary* the "confined appearance" given to it by the stone walls around the plots of land. The Spanish and French spoken everywhere sounded strange to the Virginia-born Binghams. The ordinance prohibiting hogs from "going about at large in the city" was nine years in the future, so these animals were everywhere, reveling in the deep mud of the streets.

The riverfront was the busiest place in the city. The Mississippi River has often been called the Highway of the United States. Pouring into that great river, some twenty miles upstream, was the roaring, untamed Missouri River—the Big Muddy. This river system carried the trade of the country. Far downstream was New Orleans where goods were exported to foreign markets. Many a beaver hat worn by a fashionable young gentleman in London started as a beaver pelt shipped down these rivers.

There on the riverfront a traveler might see the shaggy-haired mountain men squatting on a buffalo robe playing at Old Sledge, with a hatful of silver dollars going to the winner. There tall Missouri frontiersmen brawled in the Rocky Mountain House as they tossed off strong Monongahela whisky. There stalked the Delaware Indians with their blanketed wives. There were the rich merchantmen wearing fine broadcloth coats and ruffled linen shirts. And there a traveler could hear the wild music of a fandango, with its fiddles and banjos, and the shouts of the dancers as they swung the dark-eyed French beauties.

From the mists of ancient times the rivers had been traveled by boats that depended on the skill and muscle of men. The Indian canoes came first, then the bullboats, the pirogues, and the flatboats. They got their wares to market by oars, poles, or cordelles. Now the end of all that was in sight. The steamboat *Zebulon Pike* docked at St. Louis in 1817, having made the trip from Louisville, Kentucky, at the speed of three miles per hour. Indians on the wharf fled from the snorting puffing monster. The white settlers stood and cheered. Change was in the air, and little George Bingham was to be part of that change.

A census published in the *Missouri Gazette*, St. Louis, December 8, 1815, states that "the number of souls in town was 2,000." By the time the Binghams arrived there were more—perhaps twice as many. The big push of migration to Missouri Territory, spurred by the Northwest Ordinance of 1787 forbidding slavery north of the Ohio River, had begun to reach the frontier. Southern families who wanted to bring their slaves when they came West found it possible to do so in Missouri. They came by the hundreds.

The pride of early St. Louis was "the great cathedral." It had been begun in 1818, and years would pass before it was finished. The *City Directory* of 1821 told of its bells from France, original paintings by Raphael, Guido, and Rubens, ancient gold embroideries from France, and "elegant organ." The bishop had a library of eight thousand volumes.

In the same *Directory* is an account of the busy commercial life of the city. A few of the occupations listed are forty-six mercantile houses, three auctioneers, three weekly newspapers, three druggists, three midwives, nine blacksmiths, four hairdressers and perfumers. There was also "a portrait painter who would do credit to any country." Unfortunately the *Directory* neglects to give his name.

Another family who had come west earlier than the Binghams was the Boone family—the famous frontiersman, Daniel, and his sons and daughters. They had a big part in opening up the country to settlement.

In 1798, at the time when the Spanish still owned the Louisiana country, of which Missouri was a part, the government of Spain had offered Daniel Boone one thousand arpents of land (845 acres) to settle in the area. The Spanish knew that Boone's reputation would attract others. Having lost his Kentucky land through legal entanglements, Daniel accepted the offer and walked the whole way to St. Louis to take up new land. He was sixty-four years old at the time. The entire population turned out to welcome him. The land he chose was in the Femme Osage District. Later he became a syndic (a magistrate).

His sons, Daniel Morgan and Nathan, located a salt spring in Howard County, Missouri, in 1807. With three other settlers they set up a furnace of forty kettles for the manufacture of salt. They shipped the salt by dugout 250 winding miles downriver to St. Louis, where it sold for two dollars a bushel.

Salt was an important item of sale in the early markets, but in addition to making salt, Nathan Boone became the leader of the hard-riding force called the Rangers. These men patrolled the banks of the Missouri River from Loutre Island to Salt River during the Indian troubles in the War of 1812.

It was the fame of the Boones that gave their name to the Boon's Lick country. (Something happened to the final *e* in the most-used spelling.) A "lick" is an outcropping of salt where buffalo, deer, and elk gather. George would have known about Daniel Boone even before he left Virginia. He was the kind of man to stir a boy's imagination. Their lives touched at several points, but it is unlikely that George ever saw him. When George began to paint, Daniel Boone's was the first figure that he tried. Years later as an established artist, he again painted the great "hunter of Kentucky" in a picture that became famous.

The Boon's Lick country was rich, rolling land, easy to clear, with a deep overlay of fertile topsoil. The Boon's Lick Road was the best-known route leading into the heart of the territory. Nathan Boone surveyed it in 1820 from St. Charles to Franklin, but even earlier there was a road of sorts, called by the settlers "a trace."

Springs, little streams, and rivers enriched the country. They provided water for the crops and, more important, transportation. Bee trees yielded barrels of honey and beeswax to be worked into thick yellow cakes. Cakes of beeswax were used for cash at trading posts. Deer were plentiful, and venison hams and deerskins were regular items of trade. Potatoes, beans, onions, cabbages, and turnips were quickly and easily grown.

Henry Bingham had every reason to feel that he had made the right choice as he came nearer and nearer to the Boon's Lick country. He and others like him saw on every side rich land that seemed to be endless. All around were opportunities far beyond those they had left behind. It was 185 miles overland from St. Louis to Franklin. As the Binghams cut the distance down day by day Henry could see nothing but good in his move from Virginia. This was his chosen place; he and his wife and children would flourish here.

As they camped for the night for the last time, George sat with his back against a wagon wheel, a stick in his hand. A long-time friend, Washington Adams, said that from childhood on, George drew pictures when there was nothing to draw on but the dirt, nothing to draw with but a stick. In the wavering light of the campfire the boy drew in the earth of this new country, moved a little, and drew again. Then he stood up and scuffed out the pictures with his copper-toed boots and climbed into the wagon to sleep.

Sleep would not come. The sounds of the deep woods were around him. An unknown creature rustled in the brush; the horses stamped and snorted. Far away a wolf howled, and then much closer another howled in answer. One of the Bingham dogs barked back a challenge. Henry's voice shouted for quiet.

It was good to hear his father's voice. The image of Henry, tall, strong, rifle in his big hands, blocked out the night fears. Sleep began to creep over George. Little pictures of all that he had seen on the long journey slipped in and out of his mind. People, places, animals, houses, inns, ferries, flatboats—they came and went in the darkness. He would never forget. The journey he had taken would stay with him in the storehouse of his memory for all time.

3

Sketch No. 46
Courtesy, St. Louis Mercantile Library

Growing Up
on the Frontier

Franklin, Territory of Missouri, 1819.

To the West, to the West, to the land of the free,
Where the Mighty Missouri rolls down to the sea.
Where a man is a man, so long as he'd toil,
Where the humblest may gather the fruits of the soil.

This popular song was heard as far away as England, and it had its effect. Settlers swarmed into the western country. The *Missouri Intelligencer,* the Franklin newspaper, said on November 19, 1819: "Emigration to this Territory, and particularly to this County during the present season almost exceeds belief. . . . Immense numbers of waggons, carriages, carts &c with families have for sometime past been daily arriving . . . bound principally for the Boone's Lick."

The Binghams were among those "daily arriving." They did so, however, in July when Missouri is at its richest, most generous season. The bounty of the earth must have been encouraging to the travel-weary family as they reached the booming frontier town of Franklin.

Franklin in 1819 was certainly booming. When the whole population of the Boon's Lick area amounted to five thousand people, Franklin claimed more than a thousand of them. It was an unusual place. A frontier town with a newspaper was entirely out of the ordinary, and soon there would also be a library, an academy (1820), and a racetrack (1823).

The town was built around a square; the streets ran parallel to the Missouri River. The square held a log courthouse, soon to be replaced by a brick building, and on the west side a two-story log jail, built at the cost of $1,199. The year of the Binghams' arrival, there were also four taverns, thirteen shops, two blacksmith shops, two horse-powered mills, and two billiard rooms.

A walk around the square was an eye-opener to George and Matthias, who had rarely been off the Virginia plantation. It was tempting enough to make them jump from the wagons and start exploring before the teams were hitched.

The thirteen shops were bulging with merchandise. There was calico, gingham, and brown shirting, but there was also muslin, dimity, silk, lace, tortoise-shell combs, silk moleskin vestings, velvet, kid gloves, and other elegancies. Such fancy foofaraw might be beneath Matthias' notice, but George had an eye for color and material.

Tailor shops on the square specialized in military uniforms. They made coats for $4.50, pantaloons for $1.50, and vests for $1.50. They did a brisk business in the somber black broadcloth coats worn by lawyers, schoolmasters, and doctors. There was a goldsmith and watch repairman on the square, and of course there was a gunsmith.

Payment for these luxuries and necessities did not need to be in hard cash. In fact there was very little cash around. Trade was by means of barter. Tobacco was one of the staple money crops, and Boon's Lick salt was another. Banking had not yet come to Franklin.

As the Bingham boys walked down Main Street to the river, they passed some of the 120 log houses that were the residences of the Franklinites. Usually these were one story. A few house-proud owners had two-story houses made of sawed lumber. The handsomest house of all was owned by General Thomas A. Smith, "receiver of public monies" for Western Missouri. The general had treated himself to a two-story brick house.

On the riverfront were the town's industries: a brickyard, a wool-carding machine, a sawmill, a ropewalk to spin the Missouri hemp, and a gristmill. This last was operated by twelve yoke of oxen, instead of the water power Matthias Amend had used back in Virginia.

The Binghams may have lived for a while in one of the four taverns. This was crowded and expensive. Henry set about building a house as quickly as possible. Carpenters were scarce, and common labor got a sky-high two dollars a day. Henry, old

Matthias, and the boys all worked to get the house finished.

In his free time George wandered the streets of Franklin. He might see an Osage warrior or an itinerant preacher. County politicians gathered around the courthouse. Land speculators collected at the Land Office. On the riverfront, he could watch the boats. Down the river went shipments of beef, pork, lard, smoked hams of bear, and cooking oil from bear grease. Up the river from New Orleans came pots, kettles, guns, hoes, spices, tea, coffee, and chocolate.

Men from the riverboats came whooping and hollering into Franklin, spoiling for a fight and swigging whisky till they staggered across the square. Frontier fights were fierce battles. Eye-gouging with the thumbs crooked at the edge of the eye-socket was one of the more deadly practices. Men fought with fists, knives, and guns; duels were held over points of honor.

A boy, even as young as George, witnessed brutal fighting. One famous boast was "I'm a Mississippi snappin' turtle, have bear's claws, alligator's teeth, and the devil's tail; can whip any man. . . ." Martin Palmer, a rough-and-ready Missourian, described his fighting abilities: "I'm a raal ringtail painter [panther], and I feed all my children on rattlesnake hearts fried in painter grease." The best fighter on a flatboat was allowed to wear a red feather in his cap—until it was knocked off his head by another man.

With the house finished and the family settled, Henry Bingham made his first business venture in Franklin. He bought a tavern. Crowds were still arriving at Franklin, and there was a big demand for "bed, board, and old-time hospitality." There was always a block outside the door for travelers to dismount from a horse, and a bell to call men to meals, and a swinging sign.

Henry chose the name the Square and Compass for his tavern. He was a Mason, a member of Union Lodge No. 7 in Franklin, and the Masonic emblems were on his sign.

The first advertisement of the Square and Compass stated that the owner would "endeavor to keep his house clear of disorderly company and make every exertion in his power to render travelers and horses comfortable during their stay." The daily menu of William Rice, another tavernkeeper on the Boon's Lick Trail at about the same date, reads: "Corn bread and common fixin's, 25 cents. Wheat bread and Chicken fixin's 37½ cents. Both kinds of fixin's, 62½ cents."

There were schools in Franklin, so the older Bingham boys probably went to school here. A Mr. D. Fisher, a schoolmaster, took lodgings at the Square and Compass in 1820 and advertised courses in "Latin, English Grammar, Mensuration, and Land Surveying." He may have taught the boys, or they may have gone to the Franklin Academy.

With the tavern in operation, Henry went into another business. He and a friend set up a tobacco factory. The rich clay loam around Franklin was good for raising tobacco. The factory bought leaf tobacco and pressed it into blocks for chewing tobacco or rolled it into cigars. George became very good at rolling cigars.

And then Henry bought a farm in nearby Saline County, three miles from the town of Arrow Rock. This would put it about fifteen miles upriver from Franklin. Matthias Amend, it seems probable, lived there and operated the farm.

During this first year in Franklin, George began to copy the steel engravings he had so often admired in his parents' books. The best place to locate them was in the Gift Books popular for Christmas, birthday, and wedding gifts, and as "expressions of esteem." Reproductions of paintings by European artists were among the engravings included in the Gift Books.

George copied pictures wherever he could find them. Copying became his favorite pastime. As another boy might bat a ball or learn to swim underwater, George copied pictures. At eight or nine years of age, he did not think of it as "art training." He did it because it was what he liked to do. But training it was, and from the great masters of art.

"Much delighted with his first efforts, he continued a similar practice with lead pencil upon paper until he reached his twelfth year—at which time he had so far advanced as to be able to copy, with considerable facility, any such engraving as chance or friends threw his way." This was written long afterward in the *Bulletin* of the American Art-Union from information supplied by Bingham himself.

Copying the works of others may seem a strange way to learn the art of painting, which is an expression of originality, but it was then the accepted method for students. Even today in large public galleries, students are frequently seen copying paintings. Really, the only strange thing about it was that George began the practice by himself and for himself.

In the first half of the nineteenth century, an art school in the United States was a rarity. West of the Mississippi, there was none at all. The Pennsylvania Academy of Fine Arts, founded in Philadelphia in 1805, was the first such school; the National Academy of Design opened in New York in 1824. A few talented young painters worked with older established artists—Gilbert Stuart studied in this way with Benjamin West—but most American artists during this period were largely self-taught.

Franklin had far too much going on for any boy to spend all his time with a "lead pencil upon paper." If a term of court was in session, the taverns were full of lawyers, clients, and judges. The jail was crowded, too. The Square and Compass, with the other taverns in Franklin, was a kind of funnel through which ran the lively, rowdy, exciting life of the Boon's Lick country. It was a great spot for a boy to be.

Agitation for statehood for the Territory of Missouri stepped up the excitement. There were torchlight parades, stump speakings, fights, petitions. George saw it all.

The Missouri settlers wanted statehood, but they wanted it on their own terms. In far-off Washington there was heavy pressure from the North to ban any extension of slavery in Missouri. This outraged the settlers who were largely from the South. Most of them considered that the federal government had no right to dictate matters within their borders. They were slaveholders, and they did not intend to surrender their rights. The conflict was bitter. There was talk of rebellion, even of separating from the United States. Thomas Jefferson, an old man now but still deeply concerned with the settlement of the new western lands, wrote to John Quincy Adams: "The Missouri Question is a breaker on which we lose the Missouri country by revolt, and what more God only knows."

It remained for Congressman Henry Clay of Kentucky to devise the solution known as the Missouri Compromise. The result was that Missouri entered the Union as a slave state, but the remaining portion of the Louisiana Purchase north of the line 36° 30′ was to be forever free of slavery.

After the Missouri Compromise, Congress declared Missouri to be a state on August 10, 1821. Missourians, however, considered their territory to have become a state a year earlier, and the date on the great seal of Missouri was and still is MDCCXX (1820). These points were all fiercely debated. Early Missourians loved debate, and public orations drew great numbers of listeners. George heard all of this, watched men argue, declaim, and shout at each other. He put their expressions away in his memory, and went on copying steel engravings. Watching, listening, and remembering is art training, too, of an important kind.

In the year 1821, when so many things were happening in Franklin, William Becknell readied his pack animals for a trip that would mean much to the new state, as well as to the whole area west of the Mississippi. With his partner, Colonel Benjamin Cooper, Becknell set out for Santa Fe, which then belonged to Mexico. Men had made this arduous trip before, but Mexico had recently freed itself from Spain, and the prospects of trade tempted the Missourians. It was a dangerous journey. Colonel Cooper was forced by Indian attacks to give up and return to Franklin. Becknell got through, did his trading, and returned from Santa Fe in five months.

Franklin boys gathered to cheer the pack train out, and stood staring when the men and animals returned. George's dark curly head and Matthias' bright red one without a doubt were in those crowds. Kit Carson, bound out as apprentice to a saddlemaker in Franklin, may have sneaked out of the shop to watch. Every boy vowed to make that trip himself someday—and many of them did.

To Henry Bingham, busy with the tavern and the tobacco factory, the profits from the journey were even more impressive than the adventure itself. Goods brought from Santa Fe sold in St. Louis at five times their purchase price.

On his second trip Becknell took three wagons, twenty-one men, and cut the time of the return trip to forty-five days. So began the great Santa Fe trade. From Franklin the route of the traders crossed the river at the Arrow Rock ferry, rumbled on to Fort Osage in Jackson County, and went into Kansas Indian Territory.

George knew what was in those wagons pulled by mules with bells on their harness, and he would know the names of the early traders. They were neighbors, friends of his family, Masonic brothers of his father. Fortunes were founded on the trade with Mexico. Wagons leaving Franklin took iron goods—everything from frying pans to hammers—bright calico "of unfaded color," mirrors, silk shawls for the señoritas and silk handkerchiefs for the señors. They came back loaded with Mexican silver, with packs of furs, and driving ahead of them the Santa Fe jackasses that were bred with mares to form the basis of the great Missouri mule market.

In 1821 the Bingham family, also, had its private triumphs. Henry was to be appointed judge of the county court for Howard County the following January. In Missouri this post requires no legal training; it is an administrative position, like being a business manager of the county. For a man to be appointed to such an office meant that he was well regarded in his own county. On September 14 a third daughter, Amanda, was born to Henry and Mary, the last of the Bingham children.

But if the Bingham family was prospering, the boom that built Franklin was slowing down. The price of corn fell to a miserable ten cents a bushel; beef and pork dropped to $1.50 a hundred pounds. The rate of immigration was far below that of earlier years.

Steamboats were coming onto the Missouri River. The first to reach Franklin was the *Independence;* other early steamboats were *Yucatan, Big Hatches, John Aull, Frolic,* and *Tobacco*

Plant. Boys knew these boats by their whistles and raced to the landing to see them dock, unload, load, and steam away. Often the boats had to put in for repairs.

The Missouri was a wild, treacherous river. A description was written in 1850: "The muddiest, the deepest, the shallowest, the sandiest, the snaggiest, the catfishiest, the swiftest, the steamboatiest, and the uncertaintiest river in all the world." "Sawyers" (trees caught in the river when it changed channels) and snags (loose tree trunks and branches) rose from the muddy water to rip the bottom of a boat. Channels shifted in a matter of hours; sandbars appeared in water that had been safe and smooth on the last trip. Rocks, ice, fires from candles and lamps, were only a few of the hazards. Rivermen who piloted boats on the Missouri scorned those who had only piloted on the Mississippi. "It took a man with hair on his chest to pilot a boat up the Missouri," Stanley Vestal wrote of the river. Nearly 450 steamboats were wrecked during the years when travel was at its peak. No wonder the boys raced to the landing. Who was to say if the boat that whistled downstream would make it to the town or not? It might have to send a messenger to bring a lighter to unload the cargo miles away and free the boat from a sandbar.

From time to time George went with his family to the farm near Arrow Rock. He and his brothers could have helped in harvesting the crop or in the generally detested job of picking tobacco worms off the broad leaves. But in 1822 Matthias Amend, who operated the farm, was fishing in the river when the bank crumbled beneath him. He was thrown into the swift current and drowned. The mill wheels he had built back in Virginia were still turning, turning, turning—but the water he had harnessed so often took the old millwright's life.

The next year, 1823, Henry took office as circuit court judge. It was a very dry year. This ruined the tobacco crops and put a serious strain on the finances of the Boon's Lick country. There was no tobacco to sell in the St. Louis market. The words "very liberal terms" began to appear in advertisements in the newspaper.

The year dragged on. Without Matthias Amend to care

for the farm, it may have been left to lie fallow that year. George was twelve years old now. He was the kind of youngster whose mother says of him in despair, "He takes every illness that comes along." Croup, chills, fevers, were the lot of the children of early settlers. George had his share and a bit more. Copying steel engravings was the best way to keep him quiet. If he missed school, he was at least busy and warm.

Then, with almost no warning, Henry Vest Bingham died. His death was on December 26, 1823, when he was only thirty-eight. The illness that took him was so swift that there was no time for him to plan for his family, no time to pull in business ventures that were stretched too far, too thin.

On the heels of Henry's death, very soon after the funeral, the family knew that they were faced with financial ruin. There was little money left. The Square and Compass and the tobacco factory were taken almost at once. The judgeship was gone with the judge; widow's pensions were unknown. Only the farm at Arrow Rock remained.

Less than three weeks after Henry was buried, the *Missouri Intelligencer* announced a public sale:

> There will be sold on the 20th Inst. to the highest bidder at the dwelling house of the late Henry V. Bingham, in the town of Franklin, All the Household and Kitchen Furniture belonging to the said Bingham. Also, an excellent Gig and Harness, A good horse, A first-rate bell for a tavern, Two stoves, A Jack-screw, Two tobacco screws, A Dray and Harness, A first-rate stove for cooking, Some Cows and Hogs, Some Featherbeds and Furniture.

4

Sketch No. 3
Courtesy, St. Louis Mercantile Library

Arrow Rock and the Farm

Now Mary Bingham, George's mother, was left with seven children to support. The youngest, Amanda, was not yet three; the oldest, Matthias, a little more than fourteen. There were no relatives nearer than Virginia, very little money, and the farm near Arrow Rock.

What was she to do? A gently bred Virginia lady living in a man's world in a frontier town had few choices. She could sell the farm, load the children into wagons, hire drivers, and go back to Virginia. There some of Henry's many relatives would take them in. Or she could weep, wail, and "go into a decline," until the citizens of Franklin came to her aid and made decisions for her. She could apply to the court to "bind out" Matthias and George and Isaac Newton, who was then ten, under the ruling that they were "needy orphans." Each of these was a possibility, but Mary Bingham accepted none of them. She put her grief aside and set about keeping her family fed, clothed, sheltered, and *together.* She did this by starting a school.

Franklin's private schools were already flourishing, but their emphasis was on the education of boys. One "School for Young Ladies" had been started in the town as early as 1819. After her husband's death, Mary Bingham opened a small female seminary in her home. It was fortunate that the library brought from Virginia was not included in the sale of household goods. The books proved very useful in the school.

The courses of study Mary Bingham offered are not known, but other such schools at that time had classes in "Reading, Writing, and Plain Work." For an extra charge, students could have, "Painting in its various branches, on Velvet, Sattin, and Paper . . . Embroidery . . . Plain and Ordinary Needlework . . . Transparent Paper Lantern Making. . . ."

As the oldest son, Matthias went out to work on farms near the town. George put to work his skill at rolling cigars.

By such means the Bingham family stayed together and kept above water. They had to work hard and "make do." There was no margin of extra money for pleasure. But they preserved independence, part of their pioneer heritage.

As for George, he put aside the "lead pencil upon paper" that had given him so much delight. He had no time or energy left to copy steel engravings. His formal schooling was cut short when he was twelve years old. Because he loved to read, he still managed to do that. Cigar rolling was piecework and could be done at home. It is possible that while he worked he listened as his mother taught classes and so kept on learning.

There is a story in the Bingham family, related in a letter from his great-granddaughter, that at least once during this period George did return to his drawing. He slipped into the schoolroom and "drew some caricatures of the girl students that were recognized and caused quite a stir . . . he received a flogging for his art."

In April 1823, canoes filled with three hundred Sac and Fox Indians arrived at Franklin. They approached the town in complete silence. Then "a single voice pronounced with emphasis the word, 'WHISKEY' " reported the *Missouri Intelligencer*. The Indians came ashore and camped. "Tents were made with flags or bulrushes about four feet long and so ingeniously sewed together as to be complete protection against wind and rain." The next day the Indians put on their brightest garments and danced for the Franklinites. It was a sight to remember. George must have left his cigars that day to go to see the Sac and Fox.

Another event in Franklin was the arrival of Paul Wilhelm, Duke of Württemberg. European and British nobility frequently came to visit the land west of the Mississippi, to hunt, explore, see the Indians, or otherwise investigate the vast region. Often they wrote books about what they had seen. The Duke of Württemberg was no exception. He wrote about his experiences under the title, *First Journey to North America in the years 1822 to 1824*.

> The boat reached Franklin . . . which at that time [I] found had only two well-built houses. All the rest were only wooden shacks. . . . I received visits from all sorts of stupidly bold and

curious people. . . . My hunter requested [them] to leave the boat. . . . two people came to me . . . and requested me to accompany them to a boarding-house to celebrate a feast of good fellowship. At first I excused myself in a polite manner, but when they became more insistent and laid hands on me I chased them from the boat amid the uproarious laughter of their comrades. As this decisive procedure seemed genuinely American to the Franklinites, the affair dropped there.

And although the Marquis de Lafayette did not come to Franklin, the town followed every word that described his triumphal visit to St. Louis in 1825.

Henry Bingham's old friend, former Governor William Clark, with Senator Thomas Hart Benton, "the Lion of the West," met Lafayette aboard the steamboat *Natchez*. Auguste Chouteau, of the famous fur-trading family, and Mayor William Lane, who had fought at Bunker Hill, were at the St. Louis landing to welcome the Revolutionary War hero. He rode through the streets lined with cheering citizens.

At the home of Pierre Chouteau a splendid reception for Lafayette took place. In the evening there was a ball in the City Hotel. Every citizen of Franklin swelled with pride at the glories of St. Louis spread before the great Frenchman.

George's little-boy visit to St. Louis six years before was dim in his mind. These stories brought it all back. Clearly St. Louis was the place for a young man to go. But it must have seemed very far off as he stood rolling cigars and listening to the drone of the classroom.

Now another change overtook the Binghams. No matter how hard Mary Bingham worked at her school, or what small sums of money Matthias and George were able to bring in, the family's financial problems could not be solved. The only place left for them to go was to the farm at Arrow Rock.

In the year 1827, Mary Bingham was forced to ask the Masonic lodge of which her husband had been a member for help. It was quickly given. The records of the lodge say that "the money secured for her the farm near Arrow Rock to which she soon afterward removed her family."

The farm may have been rented or worked on shares since Matthias Amend's drowning. Henry's brother John and his wife, Mary, nicknamed Polly, had moved to Missouri after Henry's death in 1823 and settled at Arrow Rock. Perhaps John Bingham had kept a brotherly eye on the property.

The town now has the name Arrow Rock. On the early eighteenth-century French maps it was called *Pierre à flèche,* which is the French equivalent. White families had lived there as early as 1811. Judiah Ormond had a licensed ferry across the river that he sold to John Ferrell in 1818. The ferry consisted of two dugout canoes with a platform between and a little railing "to prevent the cattle from falling off."

George's uncle and aunt, John and Polly Bingham, donated twenty-five acres of land for half of the townsite in 1827. Two years later Meredith Miles Marmaduke platted the town and named it New Philadelphia.

This name never caught on. Grand Duke Maximilian, Prince of Wied, another royal visitor to the West, wrote in 1834 that "the people did not approve the name." In 1835 it became officially Arrow Rock, pronounced Airy Rock by many of the old timers. The high bluff on which the town is built is roughly shaped like an arrowhead. Wandering Indian tribes came to the foot of the bluff to gather flinty stone to make arrowheads. Both reasons are given for the name.

It was here, three miles from town, that George came with his mother, his sisters and brothers. He was sixteen, and Matthias was eighteen. They were old enough to carry on the farm work and Isaac Newton and Henry Vest, Jr., helped.

If they continued raising tobacco, all the help they could get was needed, for it is a crop that takes much labor. Corn and wheat came a little easier, and a big vegetable garden put food on the table. Hogs, chickens, beef, were all grown at home.

George would come back to Arrow Rock again and again. The town was a thriving spot. It was near one of the seven forts in the Boon's Lick country built to protect the settlers during the War of 1812, when the British raised the Indians against the white men. Cooper's Fort was the fort near Arrow Rock.

By 1827, when George arrived, "forting up" was no longer necessary. The closest Indians were a band of the Little Osage living peaceably upriver at Malta Bend. But stories of the days of Indian attacks would still be told to the young Binghams.

One of these tales was of an attack on Cooper's Fort. Colonel Benjamin Cooper, mentioned earlier as one of the first Santa Fe traders, had a message from Territorial Governor Benjamin Howard telling him to bring all white settlers to St. Louis for safety. Cooper's answer reprinted long afterward in the *History of Cooper County, Missouri* may well be quoted to show the spirit of the early settlers.

> We have maid our Hoams here & all we hav is here & it wud ruen us to Leave now. We be all good Americans, not a Tory or one of his Pups among us, & we have 2 hundred Men and Boys that will Fight to the last and have 100 wimen and Girls that will tak their places wh. makes a good force. So we can Defend this Settlement wh. with God's help we will do. So if we had a few barls of Powder and 2 hundred Lead is all we ask.

The settlers came into Cooper's Fort, among them Captain Braxton Cooper and his family. A council of war was held, and the men realized that the gathering Indians would overpower them unless they could get reinforcements. There were too few men to spare one for what seemed the certain death of riding through the Indians who were gathered on foot outside the fort. Suddenly Milly Cooper, Braxton Cooper's daughter, walked into the council and volunteered to ride for help. To the surprise of all, her father agreed and put her on the best horse in the fort. He asked if she wanted anything else and she answered, "Only a spur, father." He strapped the spur to her foot and out she rode, the story says, "like the arrow sped from the well-strung bow."

Settlers in the fort heard the shrill war whoops from a hundred Indian throats, and the sound of many shots. Milly was given up as lost. The Indians attacked again, and the battle waxed hot. Gunpowder was getting low.

All at once the people inside the fort heard the unmistakable crack of long rifles and the shouts of fellow frontiersmen. Cheers broke out in Cooper's Fort. From the portholes they could see that Milly was riding back with reinforcements. She had made it to Fort Hempstead. With gunfire on two sides the Indians sensibly retired. Colonel Cooper was right about the kind of people he led, and Milly, one of the "100 wimen and Girls that will tak their places," certainly proved it.

A popular pastime around Arrow Rock, and on the rest of the frontier, was "shooting for the beef." George watched this trial of skill many a fine Saturday. The best rifleshots for miles around came to take part, and the best in frontier Missouri were very good indeed. Men whose lives depended on accurate shooting and whose tables depended on killing game learn to shoot well from childhood. The long rifles they used were made by local gunsmiths who were always on hand to watch the trials.

When George was an established artist, he made shooting for the beef the subject of one of his best-known paintings. Sixteen-year-old George watched from the crowd and stored his mind with details.

A target was set up first—a flat board with a bull's-eye painted on it nailed to a tree. The prize, a fat steer, was tethered nearby. One by one, the marksmen made their shots. The judges decided on the winners. Then the steer was butchered; the meat divided into four quarters. "The fifth quarter"—the hide and the tallow—was most valuable, so it went to the best shot. The other quarters went to second, third, fourth, and fifth places.

Missourians were crack shots, and it was often hard for the judges to decide who got the coveted fifth quarter. Solemn deliberation took place, and there was whooping and hollering when the decision was made.

Each man named his rifle. Favored names were Hair Splitter, Blood Letter, Long John, Black Snake, and the like. Bets were placed on the sharpshooters by the names of their rifles. Betting talk ran like this: "Six bits on Old Betsy." "Four bits on Panther Cooler, first off." "Got a Spanish dollar on Ol' Sweetlips."

Saturday afternoons when George was free for such pastimes did not come often. Farm work was from "can see to can't see." He gave up his drawing and put all his strength into working the farm. A *History of Saline County, 1881,* says of the Bingham family, "The farm was cultivated entirely by the four sons who thus early became inured to toil, calculated to strengthen them for the battle of life." This rather lofty attitude of the Saline County historian takes no account of the effect upon George. The hard work was breaking his health.

Mary Bingham had started a school in her home at Arrow Rock, as she had at Franklin. Because of the distance from town, she also boarded her students. Teaching was work that she liked, although it paid poorly. The probate court of Saline County noted that she was paid eight dollars for six-months tuition for William and Margaret Lawless, minor heirs of Bradford Lawless. This entry shows that boys as well as girls made up her school.

It was Mary Bingham who noticed the state of her second son's health. It was clear to her that the hard work was too much for him. She sought and found a solution.

As George was still under age, she apprenticed him to a cabinetmaker. In this way he could learn a trade that would continue to be in great demand as the population increased.

There were two cabinetmakers in the area, and it is an odd coincidence that both were cabinetmakers during the week and Methodist preachers on Sunday. It is quite possible that George worked for both the Reverend Jesse Green of Arrow Rock and the Reverend Justinian Williams of Boonville.

Churches were not yet well established in the West. Circuit riders rode from place to place, often under conditions of danger, and preached wherever they were needed. In 1819 a preacher might earn from sixteen to twenty dollars a month, or about the wages of a hired farmhand. Many times not even that much cash could be found in the tiny frontier congregations, so it was up to the preacher to support himself. Jesse Green and Justinian Williams chose cabinetmaking.

A good deal of traveling was expected of preachers. Often they went into the unbroken forest to find a solitary cabin where one family would form the congregation. One pioneer Presbyterian missionary described his Missouri congregations: "Every man carries his rifle and shot pouch and belted knife. Most were unable to read but were *not* stupid . . . [they were] quick-witted and cheerful."

The *History of Saline County* maintains that George C. Bingham first worked for Jesse Green, and in his shop sketched his first pictures with chalk, "before he went to Boonville." Other sources insist that George went directly to Boonville and that Williams was his first apprentice-master. Transfers were frequent in the Methodist church. It could be that George worked with Green in Arrow Rock and when Green was moved to the Shawnee District, George went to Boonville to continue his apprenticeship with Justinian Williams.

Far more important than this question is the influence of the ministry and of religion in George's own life. He began to think seriously of becoming a preacher. His kindly white-haired grandfather back in Virginia had been a local preacher. Daily Bible reading and prayer were a part of his family training. Sunday meant going to church. And now Justinian Williams began to take George with him when he "rode the circuit." Occasionally he asked his young apprentice to preach for him.

Camp meetings were a big part of life on the frontier. Families lived far apart, isolated from their churches. As summer came on, camp meetings would be held with preaching going on for a week or two at a time. People came from fifty miles around to camp out and attend the services.

Families packed food and clothing and brought a tent or a wagon sheet and set up housekeeping in a grove near a stream. It was not only a religious but a social occasion. Men and women strolled through the camp, greeting old friends, exchanging news, and meeting newcomers. Politicians never missed a camp meeting. It was a good chance to shake hands and line up the church vote.

Those who planned these camp meetings tried to set them when the moon was full. Moonlight made it easier to get around, and it also created a romantic setting. Many a young man found a sweetheart as the preachers thundered of "undying flame for the sinner." Many a young lady packed her prettiest dress along with her Bible and hymnal. Marriages often took place as both the romance and the preacher were handy.

Preaching went on all afternoon and far into the night. Shouts of joy broke from the congregation as a sinner "prayed through to salvation." Sobs and tears racked the listeners as the preacher unleashed hellfire and damnation upon them. An entire congregation sometimes went into spasms called "the holy jerks" under the emotion the sermons called forth.

George heard the sermons, joined in the singing, and did his share of moonlight strolling and sharing a split-log bench with a pretty girl. Attractive girls were there in plenty. William R. Smith wrote from Missouri in 1838, "There is some tip-top first-rate girls out here. For health and girls in this county there is no better." Another young man wrote in 1839, "We have some pretty ladies in this country, and as to myself I expect to take one of them as soon as Harrison gets a seat in the Presidential chair."

Sometimes Justinian Williams asked George to preach at camp meeting, as he did on the circuit. C. B. Rollins, who knew George in later years, relates: "I have heard him tell the story that on one occasion after he had finished the sermon one of his auditors came forward and tendered him a silver dollar, saying his sermon was well worth the money."

But the ministry was not the only profession George was considering. In the busy town of Boonville he began to sense the importance of lawyers in the new country.

Which did he want for himself? A preacher's life? A lawyer's life? He balanced the two as he planed, sawed, mitered corners, and pegged joints in the cabinetmaker's shop.

At sixteen George had the dreams and the confidence that are right for that time of life. He believed in himself; he admitted no limitations; and as has already been mentioned, he had his share of "the Bingham stubbornness."

Since he was eight years old, George had lived in a world where growth, expansion, and opportunity were a part of life—a world of big ideas and bright futures. True, his father had failed to carry out the great plans that brought him West. But that failure came through death, and no man can put death aside when his time comes. George and Matthias and the younger ones in the family could make their dreams come true.

In the time and place that George Caleb Bingham lived, the rainbow arched across the western sky, and no man doubted that the pot of gold at the end was waiting for him.

5

Sketch No. 16
Courtesy, St. Louis Mercantile Library

An Apprentice in Boonville

The town of Boonville, where George worked in the cabinet-maker's shop, was much like the town of Franklin. The two towns originally stood almost across the Missouri River from each other. In fact, a popular toast "drank standing" at public dinners was "Boonville and Franklin, they smile o'er the waters."

By 1828 Boonville smiled alone. In one of its unpredictable shifts of channel, the Missouri River began to chew away at the north bank. "In the summer of 1826," says the *History of Saline County,* "came the 'big rise' in the Missouri. Water covered all the bottoms to a depth varying from 3–10 feet." Business buildings and homes in Franklin began to slide into the river. Even the Franklin newspaper moved that year to Fayette. Some residents went a few miles east and founded the town of New Franklin, which still exists. Others moved to Boonville, to Columbia, or as far upriver as Liberty.

Colonel W. F. Switzler, the pioneer Missouri editor, wrote in his *Illustrated History of Missouri,* "In the heyday of its [Franklin's] prosperity and glory and power, the long caravans for Santa Fe formed a line of march . . . merchants, adventurers, traders, and speculators congregated to grasp the wealth of this new world. . . . Nothing remains of the town except the grave-yard originally located in the rear of it, in a group of stately cottonwoods."

But Old Franklin, as it is now called in the histories, has never been forgotten. There are many reasons to remember it.

One reason, of course, is that it was the boyhood home of George Caleb Bingham. It was also the boyhood home of Christopher Carson, more often called Kit. When the famous frontier scout and plainsman ran away from Franklin and his apprentice status, his master advertised for his return, offering a reward of ONE CENT! Josiah Gregg, explorer, artist, and author of *Commerce of the Prairies* (1844), an invaluable book on the Santa Fe trade, lived in Franklin. So did John Hardeman, botanist; Alphonse Wetmore, first Missouri playwright; and William Becknell who opened up the Santa Fe trade.

What effect did the disappearance of his first hometown in Missouri have on George? Very little is known about his early life. This disappearance may be one of the reasons. The scenes of his life in Franklin had gone forever into the swirling, muddy eddies of the rambunctious Missouri River. Did this make him wish to re-create the frontier life he had known in his paintings? If there is any truth in this speculation, the effort of the artist to "find his home" was magnificently successful.

Another result, but of a practical rather than a speculative nature, came from this shift in the channel of the Missouri. Franklinites became scattered throughout towns all over the state, particularly up and down the Missouri. Wherever George went, he found friends of his family's. Many wealthy influential men from Franklin would be on the list of portraits he would paint.

But portrait painting was still in the distance. In the here and now of Boonville and the cabinetmaker's shop on High Street, George struggled to decide between the professions of the ministry and the law.

The cabinetmaker's shop was next door to Judge Dade's hotel. A frequent visitor to the shop and a friend of George's own age was Washington Adams. Years later he would become Chief Justice Adams of the supreme court of Missouri. In 1828 he was young Wash Adams, reading law in the office of Judge Payton R. Hayden. At that time, before law schools were available, this was the accepted method of becoming a lawyer. Wash loved his profession, and he tried hard to get George to join him. George and Wash and some other young men of Boonville formed a debating society together.

In Boonville there was a great deal of legal work. Land titles had to be proved. Squatters who moved onto a tract of land and demanded ownership were a special problem. New laws from the new state's General Assembly had to be tested in court.

The young debaters sharpened their wits on each other, preparing for later, sterner tests.

George took to debating at once. All the reading he had done in his mother's library, his experience in preaching, and his quick native wit were in his favor. He had a natural gift for oratory. Subjects used as topics for debate were, *Resolved,* That a man will do more for the love of a woman than for the love of money; *Resolved,* That a house burns up, not down; *Resolved,* That anticipation is better than realization.

They may have debated some of the hot political issues of the times. In 1828 the Missouri General Assembly passed a law against dueling. Anyone who broke the law was to be publicly flogged. Governor Miller finally vetoed the law because of the harsh penalty. Then there was Senator Thomas Hart Benton's proposal to dispose of the electoral college and to elect by direct vote of the people the President and the Vice-President of the United States.

Even if none of the other members came to the meeting, George and Wash would go at the debate as fiercely as if they had an audience of a hundred. When the debate was over, each went over the other's arguments, criticizing and correcting. It was great training for a lawyer. But the question was not yet settled: the law—the ministry? The ministry—the law?

While he was asking himself these questions and struggling with the answers, George had gone back to drawing. He had done some sketching in the shop of Jesse Green in Arrow Rock, using the chalk that is always around such a place. A smooth board makes a good surface to sketch on, and chalk can be easily erased. But once he moved to Boonville, Washington Adams said, George did some *painting.*

He began to use real paint. That it was the kind a house painter uses made no difference. Color was what he had looked for as a little boy in Augusta County. Now he had found some.

The first painting known to be by George was a sign for a tavern. In a letter written years later, Washington Adams recalled: "He [George] painted old Dan'l Boone in Buck skin dress with a gun at his side for Judge Dade's Hottel. The likeness was very good. It was one of George's first attempts."

It is improbable that either George or Washington Adams

ever saw Daniel Boone. If the picture was a good likeness, then George may have used as his model one of the steel engravings of a portrait of Boone which was widely circulated in the West. The story of this steel engraving is an interesting one.

In the summer of 1820, Chester Harding, an established artist from Pennsylvania, made the long journey to Missouri to paint Daniel Boone. By the time he arrived, the old pioneer was a very sick man. He lived with his daughter and son-in-law, Flanders Callaway, at their home in Marthasville. John Mason Peck in his *Life of Daniel Boone* says that Boone was so feeble that he had to be held erect while the portrait was being painted. He died on September 26, 1820.

When the news of Boone's death reached the Missouri General Assembly, they adjourned for a day and wore black crepe armbands for twenty days thereafter.

Many other artists painted Daniel Boone's portrait, but Harding's is the only one known to have been painted from life. This makes it more valuable. The artist made several replicas— copies of a picture done by the original artist. J. O. Lewis advertised that he would make a steel engraving from Harding's portrait. These engravings would sell for three dollars each. The tavern sign that Washington Adams remembered, and that George probably made using one of the steel engravings as a model, has long since disappeared, but mention of its existence can be found in early Missouri newspapers.

Does it seem peculiar that an artist's first painting should be a sign for a tavern? In George's time it was not at all strange, but a recognized way to begin. Chester Harding, who painted Daniel Boone, owned a sign painter's shop in Pittsburgh. William S. Mount, another famous American artist, was first apprenticed to a sign painter in New York. Painters were rarely able to earn their entire living from art in the early nineteenth century—they are not often able to do so today. Advertisements collected by James T. Flexner in *First Flowers of Our Wilderness* give some clues as to how American painters managed to make a living. In the 1830s they offered to do "figure pieces, heraldry, religious subjects, varnishing, japanning, gilding, silvering of looking glasses, rivers, maps, coats of arms drawn on coaches, signs, 'landskips,' pictures of birds, flowers, 'cow pieces,' and theatrical scenery."

Clearly, painting a sign for a hotel was a good way to start. It would be on public view swinging in the wind, seen by travelers. It would be noticed by the townspeople, and it would be a matter of local pride in Boonville.

Another tale of Washington Adams' about George Bingham's early painting is about a watermelon. George invited Wash into the shop to share a watermelon he had just cut. When Wash tried to pick up the knife from the melon, "the knife was not there nor the mellon and George laughed heartily at the deception."

To paint a watermelon to fool the eye—*trompe l'œil,* artists call it—is a fine accomplishment. This picture, like the hotel sign, has disappeared. The earliest-known existing pictures by George Caleb Bingham are dated 1834. But these early efforts show that no matter how much he talked about the ministry or the law, the young man's love of painting was still strong.

At this time in George's life a traveling artist came to Boonville. He was a portrait painter. This was not unusual. Before photography, before daguerreotypes were invented in 1839, the only way a family could keep a visual record of its members was to have a portrait painted. Both love and family pride were part of owning a portrait. Artists went from town to town painting portraits. They were known as itinerant painters, which simply means traveling painters. Often they had a regular circuit and came back to the same towns year after year.

As a rule these men were self-taught. Sometimes their work was good; sometimes it was stiff and wooden, without any expression. It was rare for an itinerant painter to sign his work, so little is known of their lives. It was the *subject* who was important.

No name has been found for the itinerant painter who came to Boonville about 1828. In the town most people would know that Mr. or Mrs. or Miss So-and-so was sitting for a portrait. George would have known; he would have heard it on High Street. He may have wanted to watch the painter at work, but this would not be allowed. Itinerant painters were secretive about their methods. Some would not let the subject see the work until it was completed.

But once the portrait was finished, once it hung on the parlor wall over the mantle or in the dining room over the sideboard, George could go and look at it as much as he liked. Almost everyone enjoys having his possessions admired, and the unknown family in Boonville would be no exception. It was a small favor to allow Justinian Williams' young apprentice to come in and gaze to his heart's content.

If this was the way it was, when he stood looking at the portrait, there must have come back to George the joy he had found in making pictures. The scrawls on the farm buildings, the copied steel engravings, the caricatures for which he took a flogging, the chalk sketches, the signboard, the watermelon that fooled Wash Adams—he must have thought of them all.

Was there a definite decision to give up the ministry, to give up the law, to become an artist? All that is apparent is a growing interest in painting from the time of the unknown portrait painter's visit to Boonville. From that time forward, only the need to make a living kept young George tied to the cabinetmaker's shop. He began to try some portraits on his own. None of them are now known to be in existence, but some Missouri attic may one day yield them.

At nineteen George's apprenticeship as a cabinetmaker was over. He was his own man. He decided that the place for him was St. Louis.

St. Louis was a long way from Boonville—some 185 miles overland. Cabin passage on a steamboat on the twisting, turning Missouri River cost seven dollars; even deck passage was two dollars. The stagecoach was more expensive. His cash on hand was so little that George decided to walk.

He put his belongings together and started, a slight, slender young fellow with a head of dark curly hair and a heart full of dreams. Hitchhiking was an unknown term, but he hoped to get rides with generous strangers.

At some point in the journey, George's springy step slowed. His head ached. General misery took him over. He craved water, but his stomach churned whenever he stopped to drink from a stream or spring. It was a struggle to put one foot in front of the other.

He was too sick to go on. In a nearby field was a deserted cabin. He made it that far and then collapsed. His temperature rocketed up. At last a red rash broke out on the backs of his hands and up his arms. This told him the trouble—he had measles, and he had them bad. Measles in those days was a serious illness, much more so than is now the case.

It was George's good fortune that an old Negro woman happened to walk past the cabin. She heard George moaning inside, and although she refused to come into the cabin, she knew he was a very sick young man. She brought food and water and pushed them through the door. Then she told a young doctor who came and did what he could for George.

No effort was made to move George. Perhaps he was too ill, or there may have been no one willing to take him in. Contagious diseases were dreaded on the frontier and with good reason. Daily the old woman pushed food and water through the door. The doctor came when he could, and George began to recover.

Slowly the wasting fever retreated. Now his dark curly hair, one of George's chief charms, began to come out. He became completely bald. His hair never grew back.

In some way George got home to the Bingham farm at Arrow Rock. He was a very different young man from the one who had started so confidently for St. Louis. Under his mother's care he got his strength back, and he began painting. But his hair was gone for good.

Human pride being what it is—and George had his full share of it—he got hold of a wig as quickly as possible. He must have ordered one from St. Louis or even from Philadelphia. How he paid for it is anyone's guess—an extra job of cabinetmaking, or possibly the painting of a portrait or two.

In 1831 tragedy again touched the Bingham family. Isaac Newton Bingham, George's brother, was drowned in the Blackwater River. He was seventeen.

In that same year George, recovered from the measles, went

to Columbia, Missouri, to work in a cabinetmaker's shop. His trade was useful to fall back on when times were bad. During this stay in Columbia, he fell in love with a young woman known only as "Miss S."

The sad-sweet little story may be pieced together from the Bingham Letters in the State Historical Society of Missouri.

In regard to Miss S., George wrote: "I thought her at that time handsome but I admired her most for the innocence and simplicity of her manners. We were both very young. . . . I paid her my addresses and was accepted."

Up to this time Miss S.'s parents had been cordial to George, but as can happen even today, when the young people became serious, the parents changed completely. ". . . they became very much enraged, ascribed to my conduct the lowest motives, and considered me (a 'hireling' as they styled me) guilty of the greatest presumption in aspiring to the hand of their daughter."

Hurt as much in his pride as in his heart, George left Columbia and went back to Arrow Rock.

There had been some changes in the town since Mary Bingham and her family had come to live on their farm nearby. One of these was the building of a handsome two-story limestone tavern by Judge Joseph Huston. This served the Santa Fe traders, who crossed the river on the Arrow Rock ferry, and other travelers.

Six miles west of town, Dr. John Sappington had built his country home, Fox Hall. He had earned the gratitude of thousands of early settlers and their families by his pioneer use of quinine to cure malaria. "Dr. John Sappington's Anti-Fever Pills" were made of 1 grain quinine, 3/4 grain licorice, 1/2 grain myrrh, and oil of sassafras. The mixture was compounded and sold widely.

> Quinine, quinine is my cry,
> Give me quinine or I die.

Boys of the countryside would singsong this jingle as boys today sing a TV commercial. But malaria was no laughing matter. At times a whole community would be ill of the disease, and many deaths resulted. John Sappington was a true benefactor.

In Arrow Rock, George spent much of his time sketching. When he sketched outdoors, especially in the town, he was sure to have an audience. One day four young men, friends of his, "proposed to sit to him for their portraits, taking upon themselves the risk of his success."

It was almost a dare! George was never one to back away from a challenge. He took them up on it, and "with such colors as a house-painter's shop could supply and a half-dozen stumps of brushes left by a transient artist in a neighboring town he commenced his career as a portrait painter."*

As for the donor of the "stumps of brushes," who else but the nameless painter of Boonville?

The four young men were delighted with their portraits. Word got around quickly that a new painter who worked on "moderate terms" was in Arrow Rock.

Not only were George's terms moderate, he worked so fast that he often started and finished a portrait in one day. He began to visit nearby towns and had no trouble in getting all the work he could do. In one town he is said to have painted twenty-five portraits in thirty days!

How was it possible for an untaught artist to do this work? George was not untaught, he was *self-taught*. Years of copying steel engravings had given him insight into drawing. His lines were strong and true. He knew how to observe, and his mind was stored with what he had seen and remembered.

It is part of the greatness of this artist that he was self-taught. There is no need to try to assign a teacher or a master to him. A reporter who talked with him in 1835 said, "Except those of his own execution he never saw a portrait painted in his life." Later that same year the *Commercial Bulletin,* St. Louis, stated, "No master's hand directed his pencil, no wise head pointed out his faults—he alone designed and executed."

By this time George was well started on his career. An artist's life is not easy. George's would be no exception. Triumphs and disasters waited for him. He took along to help meet them the knowledge that he himself had made his choice.

* Quotations in these two paragraphs come from the *Bulletin* of the American Art-Union II, August 1849.

6

Sketch No. 27
Courtesy, St. Louis Mercantile Library

Early Portraits

Change, progress, success, discouragement, friendship, and love came crowding into George's life in the year 1834. Of them all love and friendship were the most enduring. This was the year he fell in love with Sarah Elizabeth Hutchison, and the year he met James Sidney Rollins.

Elizabeth was eight years younger than George; she was barely fifteen while he was twenty-three. Her smooth dark hair, creamy pink-and-white complexion, and serene oval face made comparison to a cameo natural. Her letters to George are charming, but they show a very proper concern for the behavior of a young lady in the nineteenth century.

Very carefully Elizabeth did not admit any special interest in the artist, though he plainly adored her and made no secret of it. In one letter he wrote her plaintively, "But such was the cautious reserve which appeared in your manner that when I went to reside for a few months in Columbia, I could not be certain that I had made any impression on your heart."

George had known the Hutchison family in Old Franklin. His father and Elizabeth's father, Nathaniel Hutchison, had been lodge brothers in Masonic Union Lodge No. 7. There would be no snobbishness toward a cabinetmaker's apprentice such as he had found with the family of Miss S.

Horace, Elizabeth's young brother, was a particular friend of the artist. George often paid him a quarter to pose for him. Putting aside his natural inclination to wiggle and bounce, Horace would hold a pose quietly while George worked hard and fast with pencil and sketch pad.

Sketching was George's way of studying. All his life long he studied, even when he came a-courting.

One small matter in the letters between George and Elizabeth shows a great deal about the time in which they were written. Of those that still exist, all but one are addressed to *Elizabeth's father!* Possibly this was because Elizabeth was so young. At least she thought it worth mentioning on June 5, 1835, that "when father received it he smiled, and handed it to me without breaking the seal. . . ."

In this year of 1834 the very earliest existing portraits by George Caleb Bingham were painted near the town of Arrow Rock. They are of Dr. John Sappington; his wife, Jane Breathitt Sappington; their daughter, Lavinia Sappington Marmaduke; and her husband, Meredith Miles Marmaduke. An artist in Missouri could hardly have more influential subjects!

These early portraits are not signed. George rarely signed his portraits. They do have some dates and inscriptions, but experts think these may have been added later by someone else.

The four Sappington portraits are all half-length. The heads are all turned to the left, giving a three-quarter view of the face. The backgrounds are a neutral brown, but the artist has broken up the space with some lines and shadows that indicate the walls or corners of a room. Both of the men wear the high neckcloth cravat and the handsome black broadcloth coats that marked the successful man of the times. There is a distinctly lighter color on the upper forehead of the doctor, contrasting with his ruddy complexion. As he must have spent much of his time on horseback, this suggests that he wore a broad-brimmed hat to shade his face.

The two ladies have much more variety in their dress. Mrs. Sappington wears a lace bonnet with a wide lace collar to match. There is a bow under her chin that softens a little her severe expression. Life was real and life was earnest, and with nine children to rear and a plantation to supervise, the reasons for her unsmiling face can be appreciated. Lavinia Marmaduke is wearing a headdress that can only be called "a creation." It is made of many loops of quivering blue ribbons. Her dress also is blue, and she, too, has a lace collar; she also wears a gold pin and gold earrings to match. Her expression is sober, rather than severe. She was what George painted—a young matron, fashionably dressed, quite aware of the responsibilities she faced.

All the portraits George painted in this early part of his life have much in common, but each is also individual. This is one of his strong points. He was himself, first and foremost, an individual. And that was the way he painted those who sat for him—as *themselves,* as closely as he could.

With the success of these portraits and of others, now unlocated, George felt encouraged to leave Arrow Rock and try his skills in a larger town. Columbia was again his choice. He had lived there as an apprentice cabinetmaker and knew the town. There were lawyers, doctors, ministers, educators, politicians, clustered there, and each was a possible prospect for a portrait. As a young man very much in love, he was eager to make a living and a name for himself that he might ask Elizabeth to share.

The studio he rented in Columbia was on Guitar Street. A short time after he arrived, a reporter for the *Missouri Intelligencer* came by for an interview.

"We cannot refrain from expressing our delight," wrote the young newsman, "occasioned by a visit a few mornings since to the portrait room of Mr. Bingham upon Guitar Street. Upon entering our sensations partook more of the nature of surprise, than of any other emotion. A collection of well-finished portraits, each affording evidence . . . of an undoubted high creative genius."

The subjects of these "well-finished portraits" are not known. Some may have been quick studies done in Columbia. Or he may have brought others from Arrow Rock. Certainly any of the Sappington portraits would have been impressive.

The unknown reporter plainly knew a good deal about art and liked to show his knowledge. He compared George's style with some of the Italian masters. Then he turned to current American painters and wrote that the portraits in the studio "might be placed along side the finest specimens of Harding, Catlin, and Duett [possibly Jouett] and receive honor from the comparison."

This was strong stuff to give a young man just up from the country! The reporter may have realized it, for he ended with a bit of criticism: "We think, likewise, that the pencil of our artist might be permitted, occasionally, a stroke or two more of flattery with advantage. In some instances too faithful a copy of features is unfavorable to effect."

This comment might as well have been left unwritten. It

was not in George's nature to flatter—neither in paint nor with words. He was entirely in agreement with Oliver Cromwell who told the artist Sir Peter Lely to paint his picture "truly like me . . . all these roughnesses, temples, warts, and everything as you see me."

Whatever the criticism meant to George, he must have been greatly pleased to have such a notice in the *Missouri Intelligencer,* which was the original newspaper of Old Franklin, now moved to Columbia. Surely Elizabeth and her family would see it and take notice.

Just down Guitar Street from the studio was the law office of James Sidney Rollins. Like George he, too, was newly established in Columbia. His family lived there, but he had come fresh from Transylvania College, and from reading law with Abiel Leonard. Of where the two young men met, of what they said and thought of each other in the beginning, there is no record. What did begin that year was a deep and sincere friendship that was to last forty-five years. It is a friendship that has been compared to that of David and Jonathan, and the comparison does not seem too strong.

A great deal that is known about George, outside of his paintings, came from this friendship. Letters went back and forth between the two. More than a thousand letters, some people say. Many have been lost or destroyed. The roving life of an artist does not allow much baggage.

With Rollins it was different. He was a man of property and of *place*. He kept things. Long after his death a barrel was found in his home with 135 letters from George Caleb Bingham in it. These letters, preserved by the State Historical Society of Missouri, and the recollections of Curtis Burnham Rollins, a son of James Sidney Rollins, are the main source of information available to students of Bingham.

Rollins had fought in the Black Hawk War of 1832, and from that time forward he carried the title "Major." This two-months action of the United States army against the Sac and Fox Indians was one in which a tall lanky soldier from Illinois by the name of Abraham Lincoln also served. The two men would later become friends. When James S. Rollins went to Congress, he was an able ally of Lincoln during the Civil War. This had its effect on George Caleb Bingham. But all that was far in the future when the young men met.

Of course, Major Rollins was one of the first men in Columbia to have George paint his portrait. He was then twenty-two, handsome, confident, and a man of vision. The portrait shows these qualities as well as paint and canvas can. He brought with him two other young men to be painted—Judge Warren Woodson and the Honorable Josiah Wilson. Each of the three was dressed in his best—broad revers on their coats, stiff-bosomed white shirts, high stocks around their necks. Each was dark-haired, red-cheeked. When they came to collect the portraits, they made a big joke of not being able to decide which was which. George settled it by telling each man to choose the one he liked best.

It should be no surprise to learn that the next portraits George painted were of Major Rollins' mother, Sarah (Sallie) Harris Rodes Rollins, and his father, Dr. Anthony Wayne Rollins. Here, again, is the gentleman with the dark coat, but this time with a delicately pleated ruffle on the shirt front to add interest. Mrs. Rollins, like Mrs. Sappington, is wearing an elaborate lace collar and ruffled bonnet tied under the chin. The young painter excelled in these airy, intricate patterns.

Now we can have our first look at George as he saw himself. He painted his self-portrait in 1835. His face is a strong one with deep-set dark eyes. The firm line of the jaw with its rounded cleft chin hints at the Bingham stubbornness, well known in the family. He had a straight nose and full cheeks. Above the wide forehead is the crisp black hair of his wig.

Those who have seen a photograph owned by the Rollins family think that George may have painted a somewhat more handsome self-portrait than the eye of the camera would have allowed. He was indeed a young man who thought well of himself. Most strong personalities do.

In early March George again started for St. Louis. This time he got there. The *Missouri Republican,* March 24, 1835,

Self-Portrait, 1835 *Courtesy, The St. Louis Art Museum,* Eliza McMillan Fund

includes a small advertisement in which he offered "professional services to the citizens as a portrait painter." His studio was on Market Street.

This stay in St. Louis was not a long one. Breaking into the art world has never been easy, and George may have been running low on funds. He decided to go up the Missouri River to the town of Liberty, county seat of Clay County. Several former

Franklinites now living there had suggested that he come. But once more a journey brought illness to George. On May twenty-third he wrote to Elizabeth from Liberty:

"I designed to have written to you before this time, but sickness has prevented me. I was so unfortunate as to take the varieloid, a disease similar to the small pox, from a man on board the boat on which I came to this place. I have been closely imprisoned for two weeks, part of which time I was very sick, and all the while alone. People here, as elsewhere, fly from a disease of this nature as they would from Death himself. . . . because of the few remaining scars on my face I have been compelled to remain indoors . . . I trust I shall be permitted to break my prison bounds today."

But it was still another week before George could write to his mother that he was allowed to "go at large."

He found Liberty hospitable. He mentioned a Mr. Yantis and his family whom he hoped to paint. Yantis was a well-known Presbyterian preacher in Clay County. Liberty was a prosperous, thriving town. Much Missouri-grown hemp was shipped downriver from the Liberty Landing. There were plenty of well-to-do men and women to support a portrait painter.

The painting of Colonel John Thornton, once a citizen of Old Franklin, is a striking example of the excellence George had attained. The gentleman has dark curving sideburns and piercing dark eyes. In this portrait for the first time George attempted to include more of the body than the head and shoulders. He gave Colonel Thornton a thumb! If it seems foolish to notice a thumb in a portrait—and a not very well-drawn thumb at that—it must still be regarded as a sign of progress. Here, at this point, the artist began to branch out. He was no longer content with the waist-length view that had served him before.

In the town of Barry, a few miles from Liberty, was a famous stagecoach stop and tavern operated by Judge Thomas Chevis. The tavern sat astraddle the Clay-Platte county line, in order to get around the complicated regulations on the selling of whiskey in the area then known as the Platte Purchase.

Like George, Judge Chevis had been born in Virginia. This may have been the starting point for the conversation that resulted in Judge Chevis' sitting for his portrait. Cool, elegant, and reserved, the judge's portrait looked down on the farmers, merchants, Indians, and drummers who patronized the tavern for many years. Judge Chevis himself was "bushwhacked"—shot in the back—in the bitter days after the Civil War as he returned from holding court in Liberty. But George Caleb Bingham caught his face, his expression, and held them by the art of portraiture for far more years than man is given to live.

With the coming of winter George returned to St. Louis. He felt a deep urgency to make his mark on the artistic life of that city. First of all, it was the only large city in Missouri, and the first one he had ever seen. Next, it was near enough to be accessible. George may have had his dreams of Paris, Rome, New York, but St. Louis was here and now.

By 1836 St. Louis had a population of fifteen thousand. The weekly newspaper, the *Missouri Republican,* had become a daily. Itinerant painters made St. Louis a regular stopping place. The cathedral which had owned works of art in 1821 had more now. A man had been brought over from France to decorate the interior of the cathedral. His name was Leon Pomarede, and he was known as "the Parisian knight of the easel."

By 1830 St. Louis University had its own collection of pictures. Drawing was in its course of study. The chapel had fine paintings, two of them said to be by Rubens.

To this new and wonderful world of art, George came the second time. His life on the frontier had given him many advantages—some of them not yet realized—but seeing the work of other artists was not among them. In St. Louis he could look, compare, study, and learn.

As long as George stayed in Arrow Rock, Boonville, Liberty, or Columbia, he was probably the only working artist in the town. Itinerant painters came and went. He had no basis for comparing his work with the work of others. There is a considerable favoritism toward "a hometown boy" in the newspaper comments on his work. This was good for it gave him the encouragement he needed at a time when he needed it. But in St. Louis he was only one of many painters, and a newly arrived one at that.

Because he was so keen and so honest an observer, he felt sharply his own faults, his own lack of training. Inevitably he became discouraged, and he wrote his heart out to Elizabeth. This letter is one of the very few he ever wrote about his art. It was written on November thirtieth—a dreary time of year in Missouri—and he poured out his feelings, telling the girl he loved, "it is your simpathy that I prize above all others. . . .

"Though I am frequently under the influence of melancholy, when my prospects appear dark and gloomy before me, yet I have never entirely despaired, and the determination to do my utmost to rise in my profession has ever remained strong in my mind. I am fully aware of my many deficiencies, and though I generally succeed in pleasing others, it is but seldom I can please myself . . . in fact, no work has yet gone from my hands with which I have been perfectly satisfied. . . . Nearly three years have elapsed and I have yet scarcely learned to paint the human face, after having accomplished which, I shall have ascended but one step toward the eminence to which the art of painting may be carried."

Further along in the letter he says stoutly, "Whether I am patronized or not, I shall continue to paint, and if men refuse to have their faces transferred to canvas, I shall look for subjects among the dogs and cats. I can't endure the horrors of inaction."

George had no way of knowing that even as he was writing to Elizabeth of his discouragement, William Preston Clark, editor of the St. Louis *Commercial Bulletin,* was preparing a highly favorable review of the young artist's work.

Clark was the son of former Governor Clark, who had helped George's father on his first trip to Missouri; the friendly assistance was now extended to the next generation. Clark was himself a collector of paintings, and his arts column was well regarded in St. Louis. He wrote of George:

> We were much pleased with a visit a day or two since to the Painting Room of Mr. Bingham on Market-street, where we found some as good portraits of a few of our well-known citizens as we could expect to see from the pencil of any artist as young in the profession as Mr. B.

In addition to the "well-known citizens," there was in

George's "Painting Room" a portrait of Fanny Kemble, the celebrated actress. This he had copied from a steel engraving, the original painting being by Thomas Sully of Philadelphia. Clark thought this copy was "one of his best efforts." But Clark, like his Columbia newspaper colleague, added to the review a bit of criticism: "His portraits are invariably good, yet there is a want of skill in coloring evinced which does not disclose a want of genius but instruction."

When he next wrote to Elizabeth, George was in much better spirits. Perhaps Clark's endorsement had brought in some business; perhaps a letter from Elizabeth that he had read "over and over" provided new hope.

"Since I wrote to you I have been painting without intermission. I have completed ten portraits, and also a couple of buffaloe hunts of our western prairies. . . . I have now engagements to fill which will keep me busy for two weeks to come. . . . you will receive no more melancholy letters from me."

Once more George was confident, jubilant, and making plans for marriage. But having been reared as a boy to read the Bible daily, he did not neglect to be thankful: "It has been but a few years since I was a barefoot apprentice in Boonville, and I am indebted for the improvement in my circumstances to Him who provides for the fatherless and the widow. My mother is comfortably situated and is contented, and surely I should be satisfied."

George had not been alone in concern about his mother; his older brother, Matthias, had stayed at home and cared for her until her support was assured. Then in 1835 Matthias rode overland to Texas. There he joined Sam Houston's forces and took part in the struggle to free Texas from Mexico. Matthias took up land in Texas after the war and never returned to Missouri. His name, Mat Bingham, is on the San Jacinto monument that commemorates those who fought for Texas.

The upper-river towns were closely connected by trade, family ties, and friendships. George was well known in them. He was so well known that the story of his ill-starred romance with Miss S. in 1831 was not forgotten. In 1836 some busybody carried the story to Elizabeth. After five years to grow, the story was probably much exaggerated. With a wisdom beyond her years Elizabeth took the story at once to George and asked, by letter, for an explanation.

George replied that he had gone to Columbia in 1834, the period in which he "could not be certain of my impression on your heart." Not long after arriving, he was invited to a camp meeting, "which was to be held at the same place that I had left with so much disgust near three years before. I had no wish to go, but having no good excuse, and not knowing at that time why my presence was so much desired, I consented to attend. . . .

"I saw there Miss S., and a few of her friends so managed that I could not well avoid an interview with her. But few words, however, passed between us, and but a slight allusion to former times. Upon leaving the encampment I left a few lines directed to her. . . . She generously replied . . . thus it terminated."

The letter is torn, undated, and partly illegible, but it seems clear that if Miss S.'s friends thought a rising young artist would be more to her family's taste than an apprentice cabinet-maker, they were wasting their efforts. George was deeply in love with Elizabeth.

On February 8, 1836, Elizabeth wrote her answer in regard to Miss S. "I have heared it spoken of several different times but in quite a different light from that in which you related it. . . . I have now heared the truth of it and am perfectly satisfied."

From the chill of November, with its self-doubt and gloom, through the struggle of the winter in St. Louis, the year at last turned toward spring. By this time George felt that he was able to support a wife. He was certain of his love, and she was certain of hers. In April he came to Boonville. April in the Missouri countryside is hurrying streams, white flowers of dogwood, blue of wild violets, and the green haze on the hills that daily grows brighter.

George was twenty-five, slight, handsome, and confident; Elizabeth was seventeen and beautiful. The wedding must have taken place at the Hutchison home with spring flowers for decorations, a lavish supper afterward, and kinsfolk, friends, and neighbors to join in wishing happiness to the young couple.

7

Sketch No. 34
Courtesy, St. Louis Mercantile Library

Go East, Young Man

George and Elizabeth may have stayed in Boonville, or they may have gone to Arrow Rock for the first few months of their married life. At any rate, by September nineteenth he had returned to St. Louis and was looking for a place for them to live. "I am tired of living alone," he wrote her. He was staying at a hotel, but he thought his bride would not like "a noisy bustling place like this."

Such a place might have been the Green Tree Tavern, one of the best-known hotels in the city. It was located "south of the Catholic church." It had a livery stable with "faithful and attentive Ostlers. The Bar serves the best of Liquors. The table has all the varieties of the Market." The prices were "Board and Lodging by the year $150, By the week, $3.50. Breakfast, dinner, and supper, each, twenty-five cents."

George was looking for a private boardinghouse. He also needed a place where he could display his work. Househunting did not keep him from painting. He wrote Elizabeth that he had in the first week started four portraits which could be finished in four or five days.

The lonesome letters to Elizabeth stopped, so she must have joined him. On December 13 the *Missouri Republican* wrote that "he gives promise of an enviable celebrity." This was good publicity but a little late, for the Binghams left for Natchez, Mississippi, a few days later.

Itinerant portrait painters often went South during the winter months. Owners of big plantations were an excellent source of business. Antebellum mansions preserved to the present have family portraits in many rooms. George and Elizabeth probably looked upon this journey as a belated wedding trip. Steamboats of the time were floating palaces.

"Nothing in the history of travel in America has equaled

the delight of a trip in such a steamer," writes Stanley Vestal in *The Missouri,* his book in the Rivers of America series. ". . . good food, comfortable lodging, continual change of scene, plentiful company, adventure, danger, and sheer fun."

The trip to Natchez was a successful venture. The "moderate terms" are somewhat higher. Prices of George's portraits in Natchez were between forty and sixty dollars. He wrote to his mother, who wrote a friend, as mothers do, that George had been painting "with great success."

But more important to Mary Amend Bingham was the news she put into the same letter that George and Elizabeth's first son had been born in Natchez in March. They named him Isaac Newton, in memory of George's brother.

The months in Natchez brought the first letters from George to his friend James Sidney Rollins. These letters always begin, "Major J. S. Rollins, Dear Sir." So they continued for forty-five years, with only slight variations as, "My dear Sir, Dear Major, Dr. Sir." No first name, and no nickname, were ever used. The formal style of address was a mark of respect from one gentleman to another, and the passing years were not allowed to diminish it.

The first letter is a call for help. Natchez, like much of the rest of the country, was going through a financial crisis—the panic of 1837. Two banks had already closed. George's cash was tied up, and the cost of living was "exorbitant." Summer was at hand, and this would slow down his commissions. It was time for the Binghams to come back to Missouri.

"I will try and visit Columbia and if you could procure for me subscribers for a dozen portraits at $25 I should be glad to remain with you for six or eight weeks previous to making a trip eastward."

The cut in price can be understood. He had a wife and child now, and he needed money to take care of them.

The proposed visit may seem a very lengthy one, but in those days, friends who came were expected to stay. A visit of less than a week was hardly polite. Houses were large, help plentiful, food abundant. La Grange, the Rollins' country home, was famed for its hospitality.

In the same letter George urged his friend to marry: "Do *get* a wife, and *get* children, and *get* me to paint you a family group."

On June sixth, Rollins did indeed marry Mary Elizabeth Hickman. The young Binghams must have attended the wedding. Not long afterward George painted the bride.

But even in the midst of his marriage plans, Major Rollins did not overlook his friend's request for help. He rounded up subscribers for more than a dozen portraits, mostly among Columbia townspeople. The amount of time and study George had put into his painting since his stay in St. Louis was starting to show results. The 1837 portraits are more natural and less wooden than the earlier ones. The hair is better painted, and the wiglike hairline that George tended to give to his subject has become softer.

The only miniature George ever painted was done that summer. The subject was Thomas Miller, first president of Columbia College, which later became the University of Missouri. The 3½- by 2½-inch oval has a gemlike quality. Miller and Rollins eventually became law partners in Columbia.

Once again George painted Major Rollins' mother, his father, his youngest sister, Sarah Helen, and the major's bride. Plainly he took great care over this last portrait. The elaborate dress, the jeweled headdress, the long earrings, and the almost unbelievably small waist make a handsome composition. At Mrs. Rollins' bosom is a small flower, a touch George was to use again and again.

But the summer was not given over entirely to painting. In late July, George and Elizabeth Bingham bought from Claiborne Fox Jackson and his wife a lot in the town of Arrow Rock, for fifty dollars. On this lot George built a small brick house, not far from the Arrow Rock tavern.

The house is still in existence, and though small, is well proportioned and placed in a lovely setting. Because of his training as a cabinetmaker, George was able to do much of the work himself. The oak floors, the walnut doors, the "twelve-light" windows, are all the work of his hands. Tradition gives him credit, also, for setting the brick for the walls.

When the house was finished, George asked his mother to come to stay there with his wife and baby, for he was determined to leave Missouri and go East for some concentrated study. He had been thinking about such a trip for a long time, possibly even before William Preston Clark of St. Louis noted that his work showed "not a want of genius, but a want of instruction."

In a letter to Rollins, George made his intentions clear. "There is no honorable sacrifice which I would not make to attain eminence in the art to which I have devoted myself. I am aware of the difficulties in my way, and am cheered by the thought that they are not greater [than] those which impeded the course of Harding and Sully and many others. . . . I expect to be successful."

On that brave note he set out for Philadelphia.

Philadelphia was the proper place for an artist to go. At that time the second largest city in the United States, it was the first in cultural matters. The Pennsylvania Academy of Fine Arts was there, the first institution of its kind in the country. When George arrived late in February 1838, it was on Chestnut Street, between Tenth and Eleventh. The building was domed, with a pair of sphinxlike figures reclining at the top of a flight of stone steps to the entrance. Tall arched windows were on either side.

It must have been a thrill to walk up those stone steps and enter the building where all the great names of American art were represented. Nowhere else could such a collection be found. George was at the very center of the American art world.

The Academy had been started in 1805 by seventy-five Philadelphians. It had the backing of men of business, law, science, and medicine. There were practicing artists in the founding group: Charles Willson Peale, his son Rembrandt Peale, painters, and William Rush, sculptor. The president in 1838 was Joseph Hopkinson; he may be better recalled as composer of the lyrics of "Hail, Columbia!"

As to what courses of study George took, there is no record.

This early building burned in 1845, and all records were destroyed. But courses *were* available. A course in anatomy was taught by John Bell, M.D. Opportunities were given to practice drawing from casts of Greek and Roman art in the Antique Statues Gallery.

The Artists' Fund of Philadelphia sponsored an annual exhibition in the Academy building. The Third Annual Exhibition of 1838 opened on April twentieth and continued for some eight weeks. Catalogues of the exhibition sold for 12½ cents each: "Admission 25¢, Season Tickets 50¢—Visitors are earnestly requested not to touch the Pictures, the Frames or the Figures."

With what burning interest, George must have visited this collection. Moving slowly from canvas to canvas, coming back to take a closer look, squinting a little, and holding up thumb and forefinger to frame a special effect, he stored in that remarkable mind of his new techniques, new uses of color, and new achievements in perspective.

What might he have seen on his visits? Gilbert Stuart's full-length *Portrait of General Washington,* Thomas Sully's *The Tribute Money* (after Rubens), Charles Willson Peale's *Portrait of Robert Morris,* the banker of the American Revolution, Washington Allston's *Dead Man Restored to Life;* Benjamin West's *Death on a Pale Horse;* Sir Thomas Lawrence's *Portrait of John Hare Powell,* one of the benefactors of the exhibition.

There were also some old masters, including Correggio's *The Magdalene* and Murillo's *St. Francis.* Other works were by Guido Reni, Francesco Zuccarelli, and the great English portraitist Sir Henry Raeburn. Outstanding in sculpture were Giuseppe Ceracchi's portrait bust of George Washington, and Houdon's bust of Benjamin Franklin.

For many years American art had been content to take its models from older cultures, from England, France, Italy, Spain, the Netherlands, and from classical Greek and Roman subjects. The theory that encouraged this was that of "the superiority of a classic society." Pictures of European peasants might be admired, but American workmen, farmers, or artisans were not considered proper subjects.

Change was now in the air. A new awareness of national pride had started. When Andrew Jackson strode into the White House in 1829, he carried with him his campaign slogan, "Let the People Rule." The social structure of the past was weakening. The last ties with England had been cut by the War of 1812. Art as well as politics was on the move. The quiet, composed—and posed—faces that were the mainstay of generations of portrait painters no longer satisfied either the artists or the viewers. A new kind of painting was taking shape.

The name of it is genre. Because the word come from the French, it is pronounced *zhan'r*. It is a kind of painting that shows human beings in scenes of common, everyday life. Genre painting is sometimes called story-telling painting.

There had been some genre painting in the United States much earlier. The difference was that it pictured the wealthy at their everyday pastimes—riding to the hounds, gambling, or drinking each other under the table. The new generation was to show the common man at his work and play.

In this field the name of George Caleb Bingham was to become famous. As the *Missouri Intelligencer* long ago prophesied, "The country shall see with delight, and hear with pleasure, the productions and praises . . . of a Western 'meteor of the arts.' "

The Pennsylvania Academy had a famous example of genre, painted in 1826. The artist, John Neagle, was the son-in-law of Thomas Sully. His picture shows a brawny blacksmith, hammer resting on the anvil, leather apron stained and sooty, a competent, able man doing work he liked and doing it well. The title of the original, bought by the Boston Athenaeum, was *Pat Lyon at the Forge*. The Pennsylvania Academy has a replica, and in the catalogue of the 1837 Exhibition it was called *Portrait of the Late Patrick Lyon at the Forge*. But it was far more than a portrait. Neagle had caught the vitality and strength of the man doing his daily work.

After Neagle made the picture and the replica, he went

back to the safe and more profitable art of painting portraits. Far more of a true genre painter was William Sidney Mount. Only four years older than Bingham, his *Dancing on the Barn Floor* was already widely known. Mount was a fiddler who played for many barn dances. His motto, he said, was, "Never paint for the few but for the many," and his work was popular from the first.

There was another exhibition in the city at the art school of Joshua Shaw and Manuel de Franca. Twenty-one Philadelphians and painters from other cities showed their work. These two art enthusiasts welcomed the younger men coming up as artists. Good talk has always been part of the art world. George found it here.

One famous painting that Bingham surely went to see was *Christ Healing the Sick* by Benjamin West. It was hanging in the Pennsylvania Hospital. West's expert handling of many figures in this big canvas may have provided Bingham with ideas on composition.

In addition to looking at pictures, talking, and studying, Bingham was also sketching. He filled a portfolio with drawings and engravings of the works of other artists. And he bought "a lot of casts from antique sculpture," he wrote Elizabeth, "which will give me nearly the same advantages in my drawing studies at home, that are at present to be enjoyed here." He was going to Baltimore, he added, and he would then start home "with a joyful heart."

But his plans changed. From Baltimore he went to New York City. There he took to the Apollo Gallery and showed to James Herring, who was in charge, his genre painting *Western Boatmen Ashore*. It was accepted by Herring for the Apollo's fall show and listed in the catalogue.

The genre pictures by other artists that Bingham saw appealed to his restless, observant mind. Years of living by the river and watching the flatboat crews come brawling up from the landing made the choice of subject a natural one. It has been said of Bingham that "he knew the West as well as he knew his own face." So he began to paint what he knew—the everyday life of the common man in one special place and time.

New York was another busy art center, and Bingham was there during a show at the National Academy of Design. Mount had two paintings there, one so new as to be not quite finished. *Dregs in a Cup, or Fortune Telling* was the title of the unfinished picture; the other was Mount's well-known work, *The Tough Story*.

Charles Deas, who was later to live in St. Louis, showed his *Turkey Shooting* in New York that summer. George Catlin, Bingham's great contemporary who devoted his life to painting Indians, also had pictures to be seen.

Now it was back to his dear Elizabeth and to little Newton and to Mary Bingham who had stayed with them while George was gone. As he had gone East across the mountains, he chose to go home via the Erie Canal and the Great Lakes so that he might see as much of the country as possible.

The rest of 1838 and the early part of 1839 he worked at painting portraits. The expenses of even a small household had to be met; the towns of central Missouri were his market, and portraits were his stock-in-trade.

In *George Caleb Bingham: The Evolution of an Artist*, E. Maurice Bloch says that Bingham's opportunity of seeing the sophisticated productions of other artists must have proved a revelation to him: "The stiff formality of his earlier portraits began to give way to a more generally relaxed and varied system of composition." This was especially apparent in a portrait of Mrs. Thomas Shackleford, which was painted in the little town of Gilliam. She is shown almost full-face, a new pose for Bingham, with a gentle expression in her eyes and an almost-smile on her mouth. She holds a card on which is written, "To my children/When deprived of my counsel, forget not my precepts, Shun vice, love virtue/Jan. 1, 1839."

Bingham opened a studio in Fayette, Missouri. A new baby was expected, and he felt the need to add to his resources. One group of seven portraits from Fayette is still in existence. By now Bingham had advanced from the status of an itinerant painter to that of a professional painter of portraits. In the middle of May he was back in St. Louis where he was welcomed by the *Missouri Republican* with a headline, "Native Talent."

When the Binghams' second son was born in May 1839, he was named Nathaniel Hutchison, after Elizabeth's father. The baby lived only a short time. Both George and Elizabeth were devoted parents, and this loss was a great grief to them. They could take some comfort in the continuing growth of Newton who at two years of age was considered to have outlived the dangerous age of babyhood that in those days took so many lives.

Elizabeth and Newton stayed in Boonville with her family. She wrote to George in St. Louis that she was glad he had a room for them and that he intended to furnish it himself. She would be ready to join him when the steamboat *The Rhine* made its next trip downriver.

Trying to keep up with George Bingham's whereabouts during these years is like trying to watch a tennis match. Back and forth, back and forth, he went. Sometimes his family was with him, sometimes not: Columbia, Fayette, Boonville, St. Louis—and without doubt many other towns not named.

Portraits and more portraits came from his easel. Good portraits, increasingly good. One of the Rollins clan, commenting on the number of them, said, "Back in those days not to have a Bingham on the wall was as rare as not to have a Bible on the center table."

But what of the new ideas on genre painting? Were those forgotten? Had *Western Boatmen Ashore* been only a passing fancy, an effort to show that Bingham could keep up with his times?

8

Sketch No. 22
Courtesy, St. Louis Mercantile Library

Politics, Portraits, and Washington City

In the last month of 1839, George was in St. Louis, sharing a studio on Market Street with another painter. On December twelfth he went "to the country," painting portraits. While he was away, fire destroyed all the paintings stored in the studio. "All were lost," reported the editor of the *Missouri Republican,* "our own pretty face in the group."

One portrait of this period that luckily was not lost is that of six-year-old Sallie Ann Camden. One little bare foot peeps out from under her long white dress, and Sallie Ann looks happily at home in an outdoors background. There are trees, curling ferns, and a bit of water in the distance. The change from the usual neutral background marks a further widening of the artist's scope.

The winter had been one of hard work, but now spring was coming. Suddenly a different kind of picture appeared in Bingham's studio. The answer to the questions at the end of the last chapter about genre painting lies in those pictures. Bingham had not forgotten genre; he was not satisfied with jogging along painting more and more and more portraits. In the spring of 1840 George Caleb Bingham sent *six* pictures to the National Academy of Design in New York.

There were two pictures of *Tam O'Shanter,* illustrations of the famous poem by Robert Burns: Tam was shown, drunk, and on "his gray mare, Meg," as he rode up to the haunted church. *Sleeping Child* could easily have been a picture of little Newton Bingham, then around two or three years. *Pennsylvania Farmer* must have come out of the stay in Philadelphia. *Land-scape* is the first of the more than forty such pictures Bingham was to paint. *Group, Two Young Girls* sounds as if it were not a portrait, but a painting. The distinction between a portrait and painting is that in a portrait to catch the likeness of the person or persons painted is the important thing; in a painting it is to communicate whatever aspect of the picture the artist wishes to represent and wants others to see and remember.

Also in 1840 there is the first inkling of the absorbing interest that politics was to hold for Bingham. Time and again he would decide to "give up politics," but he never made his resolution stick. He always came back.

Albert Christ-Janer in his biography, *George Caleb Bingham of Missouri,* says, "Bingham was an activist. He could not stand by, as an observer, to watch the desecration of any principles which he, whose opinions were convictions, held over a wide range of interests. . . . he believed that there are a thousand ways to be wrong, but only one way to be right."

Dr. Fern Rusk, Bingham's first biographer, adds to this point of view: "He had such positive ideas as to party platforms that the Whigs, among whom he counted himself, saw in him a leader who would stand by his convictions under all circumstances."

Whether Bingham was pressed into service by his fellow Whigs or by his own beliefs, the result was the same. His temperament was well suited to politics. The times in which he lived were stormy. Troubles with Mexico loomed dark as a thundercloud. And the terrible question of slavery was always present. "A Whig, dyed in the wool," the *Missouri Statesman* called him, and so he was.

The Whig party to which Bingham and his friend Major Rollins belonged was a power in Missouri politics in the 1840s and 50s. Nationally the party was made up of several different groups. The main point they had in common was their opposition to Andrew Jackson's administration. They favored states' rights; they opposed Jackson's policy on the United States Bank; and in the East, a good many Whigs had originally belonged to the Anti-Masonic party.

Generally speaking, in Missouri the Whigs were the party of wealth and business; they were better educated than their opponents, the Democrats; they were property owners; some, though not all, were slaveholders. The river counties were their stronghold. Whigs were especially opposed to the radical or equal-rights Democrats who went by the name of the Loco Focos.

That spring Thomas Miller of Columbia wrote Bingham a letter asking him to paint a banner to be carried by the delegation from Boone County at the Whig state convention to be held in Rocheport in June. Bingham regretfully had to refuse. He was already at work on a banner for Saline County to be carried by the Young Men's Club.

Such banners played a large part in the effort of political parties to influence voters; they were made with care and artistry. Bingham wrote to Miller that "our designs are intended to be worthy of the occasion."

The banner for Saline County was a magnificent arrangement. Elaborate paintings, six feet square, decorated each of its four sides. On the front panel was a life-size portrait of William Henry Harrison, the Whig candidate for President, standing on a marble pedestal. Missouri newspapers reported that Bingham's banner was "by far the most splendid and imposing."

Several thousand delegates came to the little town of Rocheport, located part-way between Columbia and Boonville. They came by riverboat, on horseback, and in wagons, buggies, and elegant carriages. Three hundred delegates came from St. Louis on the steamboats *Platte* and *Rienzi*. On the boats were brass bands and complete log cabins to be used in the parade, and two live eagles, the emblem of the Whigs.

The campaign of 1840 was known as the "Coon Skin, Log Cabin, and Hard Cider campaign." Everywhere in Rocheport these symbols were on view. The parade was a mile long. Officials wore dark coats and light-blue scarves as they marched from the center of town to Crawford's Grove, a mile southeast. Soldiers of the Revolutionary War and soldiers who had served with General Harrison in the War of 1812 rode in carriages; everyone else walked.

"Tippecanoe and Tyler too!" was the battle cry of the Whigs. Harrison had been the hero at the Battle of Tippecanoe against the Shawnee chief, Tecumseh, in 1812. John Tyler was his running mate. Opposing them would be President Martin Van Buren and Richard M. Johnson, Democrats.

It was in the grove of sugar trees a mile from Rocheport that George Caleb Bingham made his first major political speech. He had plenty of company. Other speakers were Major Rollins, Abiel Leonard of Fayette, and Alexander Doniphan of Liberty, all leaders in the Whig party in Missouri, and all men whose portraits Bingham painted. Another speaker was Fletcher Webster, son of the great Daniel Webster.

At this convention and at others Bingham often made sketches from life. The sketches were done in pencil on rough paper, usually only one figure on a page. They were done in haste, as if he might have been working standing, or sitting on a stump; but they were done skillfully. There are no women in them; women had no place then in practical politics. At the end of a long day of speaking, cheering, and parading, Bingham would work the sketches over carefully, using India ink or occasionally watercolor.

Fortunately he kept them, pages and pages of drawings, vital and dynamic with strong sure lines. So much of Bingham's work has been lost that it seems almost a miracle that these on-the-spot drawings should have survived. A hundred and seventeen of them, possibly half the original number, were bought by John How, a wealthy and generous merchant of St. Louis, who gave them to the St. Louis Mercantile Library in 1868.

Were these working notes to be used in pictures at some future time? Did Bingham plan that far ahead? Probably so, although not much is known about his methods. But in the genre paintings that he was to produce a few years later, many of these sketched figures can be identified.

Bingham's intense awareness of those around him carried over into the drawings he made. As he worked with pencil and pad, people stared or peered over his shoulder. That his sketching did not go unnoticed can be seen from a remark in a Boonville newspaper of 1844. It concerned the woe-begone looks of John Miller, known locally as "Old Ugly," who had just lost the election for state senator: "He looked really bad . . . what a pity our neighbor Bingham was not present with his pencil."

The sketches were not all made at political gatherings or limited to quick impressions. Young Oscar Potter of Boonville posed for Bingham when he was fifteen. He was told what clothes to wear and what pose to take. Posing can be tiresome, but Potter said he was so much interested in the artist's work that he endured the boredom. Years later, Bingham would do a formal portrait of Dr. Oscar Potter of St. Louis.

At this period, although the exact year and location are a little uncertain, Bingham painted one of his most attractive pictures, *The Dull Story*. It shows twenty-two-year-old Eliza-

The Dull Story, ca. 1840 *Courtesy, The St. Louis Art Museum*, Eliza Mc-Millan Fund

beth Hutchison Bingham asleep in a chair with an open book
on her lap. Such a painting could as well be classified as genre
as a portrait.

Elizabeth had told her husband how much she was enjoy-
ing the book, and it tickled his fancy to find her sound asleep
with it. He painted her just as she was, and the combination of
skill, love, and humor make it a charming picture. Her black
hair, pink-and-white complexion, and shimmering white satin
dress are shown against a deep chair with dark-green unholstery.
At her bosom is a small pink rose. A red curtain is draped behind the chair. Red, green, and rose are mingled in the background. For Bingham this was an unusual display of color.

Years later, when the picture was being restored, another
half-finished painting of a woman's figure was discovered on the
back of the canvas. Bingham had evidently found Elizabeth in
a perfect pose, and he knew better than to wait until he had a
new canvas. He seized the moment and made a work of art.

In the 1840 election the Whigs won nationally, so Bingham
and his friends were able to rejoice. The Whigs had lost
heavily in Missouri, but the President and the Vice-president
of the United States had been elected by their party, and locally, as with politicians everywhere, they could look forward to
"next year."

For the time being, Bingham's political fever cooled. He
decided that he must find a larger city, a wider opportunity.
It was a big decision for by this time he was well established
as a portrait painter. He could easily have gone on the rest of
his life painting the faces of the well-to-do men and women of
the river towns. His restless spirit rebelled at the prospect. He
wrote Major Rollins that he was going to open a studio in
Washington City in the District of Columbia. There he proposed to paint the portraits of well-known political leaders.

Once again Elizabeth Bingham was pregnant. She had also
developed a persistent cough. There was talk in the family that
going to Washington away from the harsh Missouri winters
might benefit her health.

Off went the three of them—George, Elizabeth, and Newton, who would be four years old in March. They stayed at

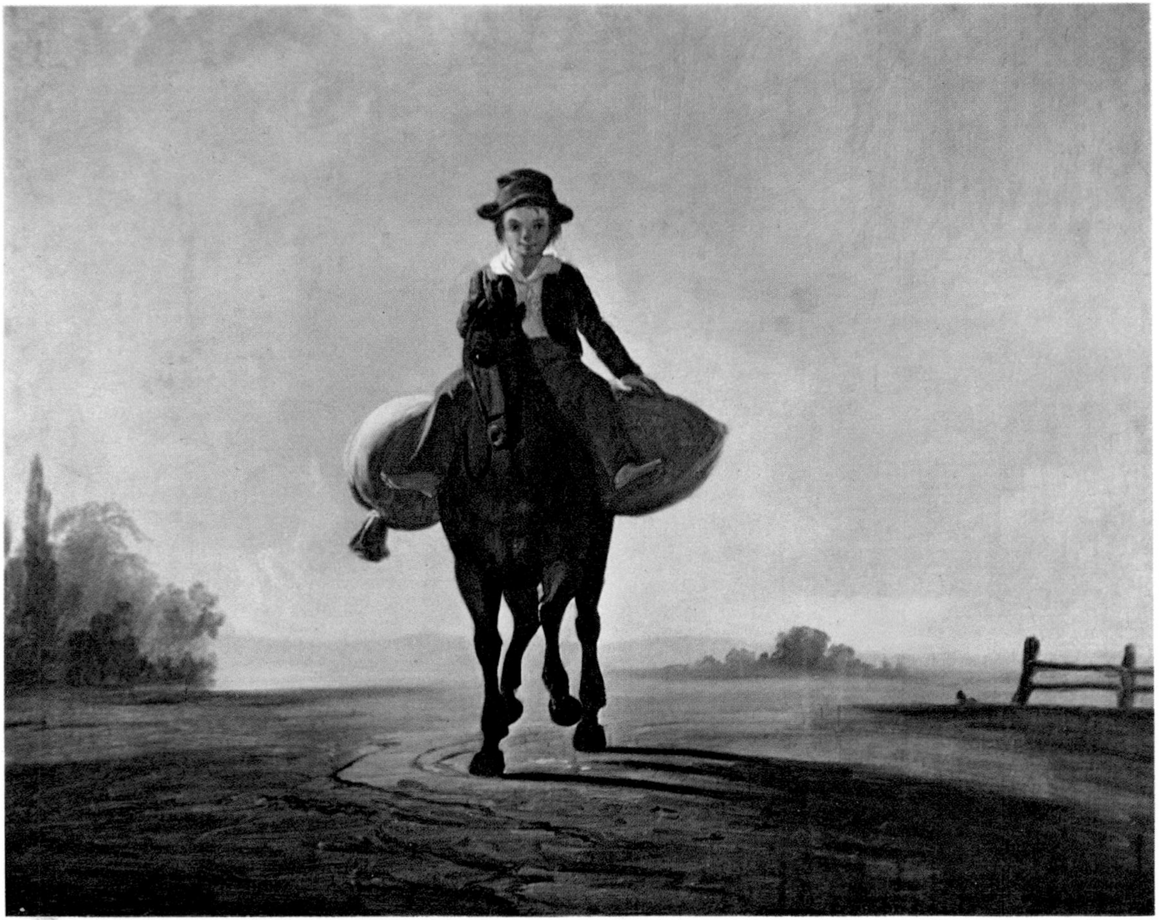

I

The Mill Boy, 1844

Private Collection

II
Fur Traders Descending
the Missouri, 1845
Courtesy, The Metro-
politan Museum of Art,
Morris K. Jesup Fund, 1933

III
Landscape with Cattle, 1846
Courtesy, The St. Louis Art Museum, Gift of Mrs. Chester H. Krum

IV
The Jolly Flatboatmen
in Port, 1857
Courtesy, The St. Louis
Art Museum

V The Wood Boat, 1850
Courtesy, The St.
Louis Art Museum,
Museum Purchase

VI

Shooting for the Beef, 1850
Courtesy, The
Brooklyn Museum,
Dick S. Ramsay Fund

VII
Canvassing for a Vote, 1852
Courtesy, Nelson
Gallery-Atkins
Museum, Kansas
City, Missouri
(Nelson Fund)

VIII
The County
Election, 1851-1852
*Courtesy, The St. Louis
Art Museum*

Mrs. Brawner's boardinghouse on Pennsylvania Avenue, "the first house west of the railroad office where the cars stop when they come into the city."

This bit of location comes from one of the letters Elizabeth wrote to Mary Amend Bingham, her mother-in-law. Like many a man before and since, her husband handed over to Elizabeth the task of writing family letters. From the same letter comes this even more interesting bit of news: "Mr. B. has a room in the Capital where he spends much of his time painting."

It seems odd that an artist should have a studio in the Capitol. But Washington was then very different from now. In 1841 the Capitol was still unfinished. Several artists had workrooms on the lower floor. It was a good place to work, to see and be seen. Morrison's *Stranger's Guide to the City of Washington,* published in 1844, mentions that the courtroom of the Supreme Court was in the basement of the north wing, "a low ill-formed apartment which seems ready to burst under the weight of the entire building."

Elizabeth was disappointed in Washington; it was not as pretty as St. Louis. There was only one paved street. "I go to the Capital frequently it is a great resort with the ladies, I have walked round the president's mansion, but have never been inside. Mr. Bingham has been all through the house and is perfectly well satisfied that there is no furniture in the house too good for the man we would choose for our president [William Henry Harrison] but perhaps little Matty [Martin Van Buren, still in office until March 4] has been packing up the valuables to take back to Kinderhook with him."

In her chatty letter she gives all the details that any mother would want to know about her son, his family, and their lives. Speaking of the food at Mrs. Brawner's, Elizabeth said, "Cakes, ice creams, mince pies, and a great variety of meats, and fowls and oysters in abundance, but I have not yet learned to eat them." All of this was served to the Binghams at fifteen dollars a week. Breakfast was at nine o'clock, dinner at four, and tea at seven. "Very fashionable indeed—rather too much so to suit my appetite sometimes."

There is a glimpse of Elizabeth's view of politicians. She

notes that of the twenty-one boarders in the house, only she and her husband were Whigs. Some boarders were members of Congress, but the family saw little of them, "as we yearly boarders prefer having a separate table from them, and a separate parlor."

Bingham kept busy at painting, although few commissions came his way at first. He was doing what were then called "fancy pictures" from the Greek myths. *Ariadne* was one. It was commended by the *Daily National Intelligencer* as "a sweet painting." He also did a nude, but from an engraving, not from life. And he painted a double portrait of Elizabeth and little Newton.

In a letter to Major Rollins, Bingham expressed his feelings clearly. "Though I have a painting room in the Capitol I know less of the proceedings of Congress than if I were in Missouri, the fact is I am no politician here. . . . I am a painter and desire to be nothing else. . . . I shall be content to pursue the quiet tenor of a painter's life, contending only for the smiles of the graces, while the great world may jog along as it pleases."

Things were moving along very well now. Life at Mrs. Brawner's boardinghouse was interesting; the Binghams had made some good friends; commissions were increasing; the new baby was expected very soon. Then with the terrifying suddenness of a Missouri River flood, tragedy swept over them. Little Newton, only a few days short of his fourth birthday, became ill with croup. On March 13, 1841, he died. The following day Elizabeth gave birth to her third child, another boy. He was named Horace.

Newton's death after a very short illness came as a deep shock to his parents. For more than a month George was unable to paint. Elizabeth was prostrate with grief, but she did have to rouse herself to care for the new baby. Their Washington friends did all that any friends could do. One letter from Bingham to Major Rollins about Newton's death has in it this touching sentence: "While he lived he knew nothing but happiness."

When Elizabeth had somewhat recovered, she and her husband and Horace went south to Petersburg, Virginia. Bingham located a painting room to rent near Swan's Bookstore and set to work. When September came, finding a little free time on his hands, he went alone to revisit the scenes of his childhood in Augusta County.

After the trip he wrote a long letter to his mother, telling her of relatives and friends. He described his visit to the mill: "After satisfying myself by going in and around it, I went on up the river. . . . I saw a grey-headed Negro whom I at once concluded to be him [Tom]. . . . I went up to him and offered my hand, calling him by name, he looked at me with speechless astonishment, I asked him if he had not seen me before, he said never that he knew of, I asked him who owned the place before Wiest lived there. Henry Bingham, he replied, his face irradiated with pleasure as the truth flashed upon him that I was his son."

Bingham stayed on talking with Tom in his little house under Cave Hill, "the pattern of comfort, neatness, and cleanliness," for about three hours. Tom confided that he could no longer work as hard as he used to do. Tom's wife, more outspoken than he, said that the white folks had worn out her husband and had no more use for him. In leaving, Bingham told Tom to let him know if he had need of help in the future. All in all it was a good visit.

After stopping to see his father's brother, Joseph, Bingham went back to Petersburg. There he wrote the account of his trip and he closed the letter by giving his mother the happy news of the new baby: "Horace is the largest child of his age in the Country, he weighs 22 pounds."

In the fall Elizabeth took Horace to Missouri for the winter. While she was there, Bingham wrote long letters to her, filled with news of the boardinghouse and city:

"We have an old quaker gentleman from Ohio sojourning with us at present, he is rich and a widower, and professes to be fond of the *Wimmen*. . . .

"Stirring scenes in the Capitol will soon commence again as the Loco Focos appear in high spirits."

He also sent news of portraits he was painting, some of which would be packed to ship back to Missouri. In February, he wrote, "The Potomac has been frozen over to Alexandria, the canals, and even the Avenues have been encrusted with ice, until the boys could skate in every direction through the city."

Elizabeth and Horace returned in the early spring. That summer Bingham was able to paint portraits for Mrs. Brawner. These she accepted to pay their board bill for the next three months. His studio was now on Pennsylvania Avenue, only a short distance from the boardinghouse. When Horace learned to walk, he would toddle down to the studio several times a day. There is an unfinished Bingham picture of a small boy asleep in a big chair. It could easily be Horace. The story is that his father was never able to get Horace into the same pose again, and so he gave it up.

Once again Elizabeth took over the writing of family letters. Now her words are not so encouraging. "Mr. Bingham is as much devoted to his profession as ever but he is not making as much clear of expenses as I would wish him to be. He is completely wedded to this city. I cannot imagine what has kept us here so long." The letter has a homesick sound. Here in the excitement of Washington, where the great men of the nation congregated, did she long for Arrow Rock and Boonville?

Among the well-known men of the day painted by Bingham during his years in Washington were Daniel Webster, John Quincy Adams, and John Howard Payne.

The portrait of Webster looks out from deep-set eyes as if the famous orator were about to begin one of his great speeches. It is truly "a speaking likeness." Contrary to his usual practice, the artist put on the back of the canvas, "Likeness of Dan'l Webster from life by George C. Bingham, 1844."

A good many stories have gathered about the portrait of John Quincy Adams, sixth President of the United States, and in 1844 a member of Congress from Massachusetts. Adams, a tireless keeper of diaries, wrote: "From half past 9 o'clock I sat to Mr. John Cranch and Mr. Bingham who occupy jointly the painting room for my portrait." He listed five more sittings, and on May twenty-first gave his opinion that "neither . . . is likely to make out either a strong likeness or a fine picture." On May twenty-ninth he wrote that Bingham had already finished.

The small picture was painted on a walnut board. When completed it was given to Major Rollins and dated, as was Webster's, 1844. Bingham made three portraits of Adams, but this is the earliest. Mr. Adams' pessimistic remark on the painters may come from his having sat for forty-five artists in his lifetime. He wondered in his diary if "another man lives who has been so woefully and so variously bedaubed as I have been." Whatever the opinion of the original, one who looks at the picture is struck by the character of the old statesman; the sternness of the face, the penetrating eyes, give the impression of life.

Of John Howard Payne, author of "Home, Sweet Home," C. B. Rollins relates that he liked to drop in at the studio and watch Bingham work. He chose a small chair, leaned one arm on the chair back, and propped his head on his hand. This is the way Bingham painted him. It is the only portrait he ever did in watercolor. On the lower edge is written, "The Author of 'Home Sweet Home,' presented by John Howard Payne to G. C. Bingham."

Another notable painted at this time is known through one of Elizabeth's letters to Mary Bingham. John Tyler was now president, as William Henry Harrison had lived only thirty-one days after his inauguration. Tyler had his son, Robert Tyler, as his secretary. Bingham painted Robert Tyler, according to Elizabeth, and "succeeded admirably."

Whatever the reasons, personal, financial, or professional, the Binghams returned to Missouri in 1844. Almost at once the old lure of politics began. Major Rollins asked his friend to make a banner for the Boone County delegation for the Whig convention in Boonville. Bingham agreed to do so if he might paint the banner on linen, "the only material on which I can make an effective picture." At the same time he was working on similar banners for Howard and Cooper counties.

These banners were two-sided, rather than four-sided. Even so the artist must have worked hard to finish them. Rollins' request was dated September 23; the convention was to begin October 10.

Six pictures about six by seven feet, to be carried by four to six men were painted by Bingham for the convention. He charged fifty to sixty dollars each. Howard and Cooper counties had full-length portraits of Henry Clay, great man of the Whig party. For Boone County Bingham proposed painting Daniel Boone in deadly combat with an attacking Indian. The reverse side of the Howard County banner showed a large buffalo "making the poke stalks fly to the right and the left . . . ," a political pun on the name of the Democratic candidate, James K. Polk.

What a convention it was! It started at sunrise with a cannon salute. The town was cram-jammed with delegates. More party members came pouring in from every direction. Soon the street was a mass of cheering people, leaving room only for the parade. Delegates marched in double file, "amid the smiling countenances and white handkerchiefs that were waved from the windows . . . by the innocent, virtuous, and fair Whig ladies," wrote the Boonville *Observer*.

The biggest of all the counties was Howard, and its delegation marched with pride, carrying on its banner painted by Bingham, the life-size portrait of the Whig candidate, Henry Clay. Cooper County was close behind with a similar design.

Bingham's third banner, the most interesting, survives in part today (Color Plate I). It was painted for the Boonville Juvenile Clay Club, a group of enthusiastic young Whigs. On one side is a boy riding through the "slashes" on a pony. He has a sack of grain for a saddle and is plainly going to the mill. "Slashes" is a rural southern term for swampy ground, and the whole thing illustrated the political tag for Clay, "The Millboy of the Slashes." The reverse had a picture of a boy carving the name "Henry Clay" into a rock.

Ninety-nine years later, in 1945, Professor Bloch, then of the Faculty of Art at the University of Missouri, discovered the banner in Columbia. It was in a poor state of preservation, but still recognizable. It has been restored and today it marks an addition to the growing number of Bingham's early genre paintings.

Although as a poster it had a political significance, it can be looked on as a picture, too. A young boy is going about his daily tasks. He rides forward on his small dark pony against a summer blue sky. The grain sack sags in the middle, the boy's bare feet toe outward, the battered round straw hat perches jauntily on his head. It all makes a single impression. No wonder the local newspaper hailed it as a "most beautiful banner . . . painted by Mr. Bingham, a noble young artist of this city."

Alas for the other Bingham banners! The one for Cooper County was destroyed by fire somewhat later. But the one for Howard County had a worse fate. The Boonville *Observer* relayed the story, October 15: "Some villains went into the courthouse where the whig banners were placed and cut several gashes in the portrait of Mr. Clay. . . . One gash several inches in length was cut across the throat."

9

Sketch No. 1
Courtesy, St. Louis Mercantile Library

Genre Paintings

From the first page of this book, George Caleb Bingham has been called "the Missouri artist." On his return from Washington he began to be called by that title in Missouri newspapers. Pride in his work and in the famous men he painted spread over the state. So far he was still thought of only as a portraitist. This is understandable. His portraits were seen and known; his genre work was sent East, and it was, as yet, a small amount in comparison with the portraits.

For a season Bingham set up his studio in Jefferson City, capital of the state. As in Washington, his painting room was in the actual capitol building. Members of the General Assembly came and went past his door.

A new frontier was opening in the Northwest. The trail to Oregon was choked with emigrants. An editor in Independence, Missouri, saw them passing the door of his shop and wrote: "Now comes team after team, each drawn by six or eight stout oxen, and such drivers . . . not one of them less than six feet two in his stockings. Whoo-ha! Go it boys! We're in a perfect Oregon fever."

A Boonville editor was more pessimistic: "Nine out of ten of these Texas and Oregon emigrants will wish they were back in Missouri before one year rolls by."

Plank roads were the newest craze in the 1840s, and Missouri was trying to pull out of the mud. Roads were eight to twelve feet wide, covered with sawed planks. At one time fifty companies were in the business. These were toll roads which made travel expensive, but the choice was mud over the boot tops *when you sit in the saddle,* as frontier jokers insisted. However, the planks rotted and warped, and the whole scheme was abandoned.

Eighteen forty-five is the true beginning of the great genre paintings by which Bingham will be remembered. For ten years he would paint a profusion of people, rivers, courthouses, rivermen, politicians, watermelons, drunks, checker players, flatboats, dogs, and the dusty streets of little western towns. He painted them with strength and vitality, a record of the life of his time.

The first and perhaps the finest is *Fur Traders Descending the Missouri*. It shows two traders in a pirogue gliding down the river carrying the season's catch of furs to market. The boat is made from a hollowed out log, and it rides low in the water. At one end is the old trader, his paddle dug into the stream. He wears a red-striped shirt which is repeated in the blue-striped shirt of the same pattern of the young boy leaning on the bale of furs. The original title was *French Trader and His Half-Breed Son,* so the boy must be the product of one of the many marriages between a French *coureur du bois* and an Indian woman. At the other end of the pirogue a small black animal is chained to the prow. The glassy surface of the water reflects the whole scene. Mist rises behind the trader and enfolds the small island in a dreamlike quality. Pink and gold clouds drift across a pale blue sky. Snags rise from the bottom of the river, dangerous and shifting. (Color Plate II)

So well has the artist painted that the viewer can fairly smell the river. In this picture the very essence of time past was put onto the canvas by a man who knew and loved what he painted. Professor McDermott wrote: "Had it been his sole work to survive, we would yet know its author to be a grand painter."

But what is that "small black animal"? It is a question that has been asked often. Bingham never identified the creature. A variety of others have tried. A cat, a fox, a bear cub? One young girl looking at a print of the picture insisted it was an owl.

Cats were valuable in the fur trade as protection against rats and mice that could destroy a season's catch of furs, but they were usually kept at warehouses. Those who have seen a close-up detail often vote for "fox" because of the sharp-pointed nose. The Metropolitan Museum of Art in New York, owners of the picture, took a scientific approach and said, "We have the word

of the American Museum of Natural History that our little
chained creature is more like a fox than anything else, bear being out of the question."

Yet a strong vote for "bear cub" comes from McDermott
who states, "The bear cub chained in the bow of the dugout
(*not* a cat, *not* a fox, but plain for all with eyes to see, a bear cub
brought down from the mountains)."

Another solution is that the small black animal is a mystery,
intended as such by the painter. To each let it be his own creature—cat, fox, bear cub, or even owl. It came from a far place,
unknown and unknowable; it is a part of the mist smoking from
the river, the distant dreamlike shore. John Demos writing in
the *American Quarterly* puts it this way: "Perhaps Bingham
purposely contrived it thus, so as to dramatize the feelings of
wonder, or puzzlement, of both envy and suspicion with which
Missouri townfolk would regard these fur traders."

In Bingham's sketches can be found the two figures in the
dugout. The man in the sketch is younger than the man in the
picture, but the boy in the picture is younger and sleeker than
the boy in the sketch.

Fur Traders Descending the Missouri was submitted to the
American Art-Union in New York, along with three other Bingham pictures. The American Art-Union was an unusual organization, and one to which Bingham, by his own statement, owed
much. It was organized in 1838. Dues were five dollars a year.
The purpose as stated was "a philanthropic and patriotic desire
to foster American Art."

The fostering of art was to be done by financial encouragement, and by educating the public in artistic matters. From the
membership fees, works of art were bought. Some of those
chosen were engraved. A steel engraving was sent to each member each year. An original painting was then distributed "by lot,
each member having one share for every five dollars paid by
him."

The parent organization of the American Art-Union was
the Apollo Art Gallery in New York. This was the place where
Bingham took his first genre work, *Western Boatmen Ashore,*
so his name was known to them. The American Art-Union came

into being at a fortunate time. National pride was blossoming. Writers had already whetted the country's appetite with stories of the western frontier. Washington Irving and James Fenimore Cooper were only two in a long list of authors. A made-to-order audience had been created for painters of the West. By 1849 the Art-Union had 18,690 members, a sizable number for any organization of artists to reach.

Fur Traders Descending the Missouri, The Concealed Enemy, Cottage Scenery, and *Landscape* were the four pictures Bingham sent. All four were accepted. In the annual distribution by lottery, *Fur Traders* went to a subscriber in Mobile, Alabama; *Concealed Enemy,* a not too successful picture of an Osage warrior crouching by a rock, went to Pittsburgh, Pennsylvania; *Cottage Scenery* was won by a member in Macon, Georgia; *Landscape*'s destination is not known.

The Art-Union accomplished for American artists a wide scattering of their original works which was much to their advantage. In addition to the paintings won in the lottery, and the steel engravings for each member, the *Bulletin* published the biographies of the artists and comments on their work. Much of what is known about Bingham comes from these *Bulletins.*

Bingham was delighted with the success of his genre paintings. He began to spend more and more time with what the newspapers called "his new line." Some portraits are in this period, but not many. Now he had four more pictures in preparation for the Art-Union. "The Missouri artist" had hit his stride!

On March 15, 1845, Clara, the Bingham's first daughter, was born. A year later George was still working to get his four pictures off to the Art-Union. They were first exhibited in St. Louis where they were praised as being "really capital paintings."

Boatmen on the Missouri, Interior, Landscape with Cattle (Color Plate III), and *The Jolly Flatboatmen* were sent to New York in 1846. Of the four *The Jolly Flatboatmen* was to be by far the best known. It is one of Bingham's most popular paintings. Later he made two other versions (Color Plate IV).

The original of *The Jolly Flatboatmen* was chosen to be engraved by the Art-Union. At least eighteen thousand engravings were sent out to members. Bingham was paid $290 for the painting, a big increase over his earlier prices, but the engraver received $3,374.70 for his work!

The original title was *Dance on the Flatboat*. It is a happy, vigorous subject. Only a sour soul could look at it and not feel like smiling. Some men on a flatboat on the river have stopped in the work of the day as one of them dances to the tunes scraped on a fiddle and banged out on a skillet. The dancer flings his arms into the air as he jigs for the sheer joy of living.

In sober truth the work of flatboatmen was hard, rough, dangerous, and poorly paid. Perhaps that is the reason they had such a good time when they were able to do so. The mood of the picture is that tomorrow does not exist; the moment is to-day; the fun is *now*.

Bingham saw such boats at least once a day in Franklin, or in Arrow Rock. He painted the boat and the crew as he saw them—not daredevils, not river rats, not adventurers, but men taking a break in a day of hard work. This is true genre.

For all the carefree abandon of the flatboat crew, the artist went about painting them with the greatest care. The glassy river, the shady shores, create the scene. The picture is one of the best examples of Bingham's use of the classic pyramid composition. The waterline of the flatboat which runs straight across the lower edge, with only a little strip of water to reflect an image and a touch of blue, makes the base of the pyramid. The work-men are so placed above the base that the dancer is the central figure, the apex. Space is left around him to show the action of his body. He is a little off-center for overmuch symmetry is bad composition. Below the dancer are the musicmakers, each with enough space to show their action with fiddle and skillet.

Instruction books for artists in the 1800s insisted on proper composition. Bingham used the rules they laid out. The pyra-mid can be seen in his pictures over and over. It was not a new idea. Leonardo da Vinci had used it in 1485 in *The Virgin of the Rocks,* and so had other artists forward and backward in time. Bingham was aware of the rules of composition; he studied them, knew them, and above all, adapted them into his own style.

Raymon and Waring's Great Zoological Exposition from New York came to Boonville and Arrow Rock in 1846. Admission was thirty cents, children and servants half-price. In the Grand Cavalcade was "an Elephant in Harness, a Camel, a Buffalo, 8 Monkies, a Cassowary, a Lion, a Tiger, and Wolves." Bingham was thirty-five that year. Not too old to like a circus, and not too busy, hopefully, to take little Horace.

As he gazed at "a Buffalo" he may have marveled at the changes in the country. He had come to Missouri in a time when buffalo meat and buffalo robes were a regular part of life, not curiosities.

In the spring of 1846 Bingham's political fever that had been quiet for some time began to rise. He went to Columbia to talk things over with Major Rollins, a power in the Whig party. With the major's backing he decided to enter actively into politics. In June he was nominated as Whig candidate for the state House of Representatives from Saline County.

On the Democratic ticket for the same office was Erasmus Darwin Sappington, whose portrait Bingham had recently painted. He was the son of Dr. John Sappington and an experienced politician.

Bingham went into the campaign, as he went into everything else, with all his might. He made speeches; he sought out voters; he shook hands. The voting was close. When the results were announced, Bingham won the election *by three votes*. He took his seat in the House of Representatives and was appointed to some standing committees.

To lose by three votes was too much for Sappington to accept. He contested the election. Bingham suggested that the vote be taken over, and if he were to lose by so much as one vote he would give up the office. Sappington turned down the offer, preferring to throw the decision into the House of Representatives. His preference is easy to understand for the House had seventy-seven Democrats and only twenty-three Whig members.

Sappington chose B. F. Stringfellow for his attorney; Bingham chose to be his own attorney. He put to use his early study of law, and spent time and money gathering evidence.

Stringfellow made a speech to the House that lasted several

hours. Bingham's answer was at least as long. The Boonville *Observer* said of the artist-politician that he "salted down the whole Sappington family . . . scattered red-hot shot in every direction. . . ."

The House took three days to consider the matter and on the eighteenth of December announced that Sappington was elected.

It was a painful defeat. But it was out of this experience, bitter though it was, that Bingham got the hard-won knowledge which made his future paintings of the political scene authentic to the last degree. He had been there and *he knew*.

"I have been," he wrote to Major Rollins, "for the last four months full waist deep in LocoFocoism. . . . An Angel could scarcely pass through what I have experienced without being contaminated. *God help poor human nature.* As soon as I get through with this affair, and its consequences, I intend to strip off all my clothes and bury them, scour my body all over with sand and water, put on a clean suit, and keep out of the mire of politics *forever.*"

10

Sketch No. 65
Courtesy, St. Louis Mercantile Library

Elizabeth and Eliza

After his humiliating political defeat, Bingham went back to Arrow Rock and started work on a new picture, *Raftmen Playing Cards*. Cards were popular with rivermen. The game in the picture is Three-Up. Two players are sitting on a long bench, and one has just put down an ace; according to the *Missouri Republican,* the other man is worrying about what to play next. Other raftmen are standing around ready to give advice. At the far end of the raft the only working member of the crew poles the raft along. It is a relaxed, easy-going picture.

A raft of this kind was not meant to carry a lot of cargo but was itself part of the cargo. Lumber cut and sawed upstream was bound together in "flats" and floated downriver in the spring rise. The current moved it along. The crew carried long poles to guide the raft away from sandbars or riverbanks. At the end of the trip in some port city like New Orleans, the raft was broken up and the lumber sold. Huckleberry Finn and Jim, the runaway slave, went down the Mississippi on such a raft in Mark Twain's great story.

A long article in the *Missouri Republican* was devoted to *Raftmen Playing Cards* when it was on display at Wool's Store in St. Louis. A sentence from that article sums up the effect of these river pictures. "To look at any of his pictures is but to place yourself on board one of the many crafts which float upon our streams."

At Wool's Store in November was exhibited another genre painting which begins Bingham's great series of political pictures. The title is *The Stump Orator*. Although the picture has disappeared, a description of it, and a daguerreotype still exist. The orator is mounted on the stump of a just cut tree. His opponent, angry and ready to give him "what for," waits for his chance. Around the trunk of the felled tree are about sixty men, listening to the orator. Before it left Wool's Store to go to the

Raftsmen Playing Cards, 1847 *Courtesy, The St. Louis Art Museum*

Art-Union, Missourians who knew Bingham's career in politics had "identified" many of the men in the picture. He denied his intention to show actual men, but the rumors persisted.

A third picture, more historical than genre, was *Captured by Indians*. The canvas is signed "Geo. Bingham, 1848." and this makes it unusual. By a campfire a white woman and her sleeping child are guarded by Indians. Two of the Indians are asleep but the third is alert, head turned, as at an approaching footstep. Such incidents were dreaded on the frontier, although some who were captured by Indians preferred to stay with their captors rather than return to the white settlements. The picture is not Bingham at his best.

Eighteen forty-eight was not a good year for Bingham paintings. It did, however, mark the end of his retirement from politics "forever." Writing to Major Rollins from Arrow Rock, he said, "Judging from the resolutions adopted by the meeting, I think we will either conquer in the next campaign *or split our breeches*. Which do you think?"

The Whig state convention was again held at Boonville. Bingham was a speaker, and he was urged to run for the House of Representatives again, with the same opponent, Erasmus Darwin Sappington. He accepted the challenge, and he won by twenty-six votes. There was no contest this time; Bingham was vindicated.

Just before the start of the campaign in April, another son was born to the family. He was named Joseph Hutchison Bingham, after Elizabeth's brother.

The cough Elizabeth had had so long grew worse. Tuberculosis was more common in that day than it is now, though it went by the name "consumption." Doctors told Bingham that his wife's life was in danger, but they could offer no remedy. Nothing could check the wasting disease.

On the twenty-ninth of November, 1848, Elizabeth the beautiful, the gentle, the loving wife of George Bingham for twelve years died in Arrow Rock. In a few weeks the baby, Joseph Hutchison, followed his mother in death.

Bingham's grief and despair can better be imagined than described. His mother tried to comfort him, but she could not. He wanted to resign from the House and withdraw from all social contact with people. Major Rollins talked him out of resigning for he knew work was necessary for Bingham to keep his mental balance. The General Assembly convened in 1849. In his position as representative, Bingham worked hard and tried to forget his grief.

Even this early the threat of the Civil War was over the nation. Bingham, in this session of the General Assembly, is said to have made the first speech against secession ever given in Missouri. He pledged himself to stand by the Union "come what may, whether prosperity, or adversity, weal or woe. . . ."

After the session was adjourned, Bingham returned to

Arrow Rock. He painted a good many genre pictures, only the titles of which are left: *Country Politician; St. Louis Wharf; Wood Yard on the Missouri; Raftmen on the Ohio;* and *The Jolly Flatboatmen* (2).

Watching the Cargo is one that has survived. A steamboat has been wrecked on the river and her cargo unloaded on a point of land. Three men from the boat have been set to keep watch. One of them blows hard on a driftwood fire to get it going and dry out the bales of cloth rescued from the steamboat. In the distance the wrecked steamboat is listing heavily.

But in spite of politics and paintings, Bingham was still beset with melancholy. In an effort to divert his mind, his mother invited his younger brother, Henry Vest Bingham, Jr., and his wife and three daughters to come from Texas for a visit.

The visitors came, but in the late summer and fall there also came an epidemic of the dreaded cholera. It was spread by the crowds of gold-seekers passing through the country in the Gold Rush of '49. More than five thousand people on the trails are estimated to have died of cholera that year. Among the victims was Henry's wife, Sarah Vaughan Bingham, and their three daughters, Mary I., Susan, and Sarah E.

Blaming himself bitterly for the tragedy, and still grieving for Elizabeth, Bingham wandered about Arrow Rock. He was stricken with the thought that he had brought disaster on those he loved. Even his faith in God was shaken.

Into this dark valley came James Rollins. He urged Bingham to find new scenes, go East, open a studio, and make new friends in some far city. It was the kind of counsel Bingham needed, and Rollins was probably the only one he would have listened to.

In Cincinnati, Ohio, an organization had been formed on lines like that of the Art-Union. The name was the Western Art Union. Bingham sent them some pictures, and on his way to New York, he stopped in Cincinnati. He took some of his genre paintings including *Wood Yard on the Missouri,* which the Western Art Union described as "a scene that cannot be mistaken by anyone who has traveled on the Western waters."

As Bingham used the theme of the wood yard several

times, it may be explained that a wood yard has the same relation to a steamboat that a filling station has to a truck. Steamboats used enormous amounts of wood for fuel. Farmers brought loads of wood, chopped to the proper lengths, to wood yards along the river. Or to wood boats that delivered the fuel right to the steamboat.

It was July when Bingham arrived in New York, and opened a studio at 115½ Grand Street. The secretary of the Art-Union, Andrew Warner, wrote, "We like him quite as well as a man as we do as a painter." In the October *Bulletin,* Bingham spoke of his debt to the Art-Union. He stayed in New York through August. In September he came back to Columbia.

There he met and married Eliza Thomas. She was an attractive, well-educated young woman of considerable social poise. In many ways she was like his first wife, even to her name which was Elizabeth. Bingham, however, chose to call her Eliza, and so in time did most people.

Eliza's father was the Reverend Dr. Robert Stewart Thomas, a Baptist minister. Bingham painted his portrait and also that of his wife, Elvira. Two more family portraits of the Thomases were done in 1849–1850. Bingham also painted a portrait of his new bride.

All of this painting of portraits was no doubt gratifying to Eliza and her family. But the love his two children, Horace and Clara, had for their new stepmother must have been a greater joy to Bingham. It was a good and fortunate marriage.

More portraits may be assigned to 1850. One is of Vestine Porter. It was painted in Independence, where she lived and where she later married an early mayor. The portrait is an oval and the eyes look directly at the viewer, a change from the rectangles and three-quarter faces Bingham usually painted. A pink rose is at the collar of the young lady's prim white dress. The background has a suggestion of a landscape. Sallie Ann Camden's portrait had such a background. Bingham used the arrangement more and more in the 1850s.

The Woodboat (Color Plate V), *The Squatters,* and *The Checker Players* were three genre paintings of 1850. Each had some difficulty in finding acceptance at the Art-Union. In the case of the first two, Bingham cut his price from $200 to $125.

Each of these pictures is now in a public museum. *The Woodboat* is in the City Art Museum of St. Louis. *The Squatters* belongs to the Boston Museum of Fine Arts. *The Checker Players* is in the Detroit Institute of Art.

That summer Bingham reached into his memories of early Franklin and Arrow Rock days and produced one of his finest genre paintings—*Shooting for the Beef*. The picture has "life-like fidelity," declared the *Missouri Republican*. "Indeed it seems an incarnation rather than a painting, and gives us reason to exult in the genius of Bingham, a native artist of our own state." (Color Plate VI)

Already the frontier was moving westward. Such a scene as Bingham pictured was no longer a customary weekly happening, but here in the painting it has all been recaptured—the backwoodsmen with their long rifles, the log cabin marked POSTOFFICE GROCERY, the dogs, the target set up to be shot at, and of course, the well-fattened steer, the prize. Only the crack of the long rifles must be imagined.

Shooting for the Beef was accepted by the American Art-Union for the sum of $350. But the Art-Union was having problems with the New York lottery laws. No longer would it be allowed to hold the annual distribution of an original painting "by lot." In 1852 *Shooting for the Beef* with many other Art-Union pictures was sold at auction.

Toward the end of the year Bingham and Eliza came to New York. Before leaving home, he had painted a number of landscapes, and "landscapes with cattle," sometimes called "cow pieces." Some were sold to the Western Art Union, some to the Philadelphia Art Union, and a few went to the American Art-Union, which was still doing business.

In New York Bingham had word of the birth of a son to Major Rollins and his wife. On March 30, Bingham wrote, "I feel I assure you, not a little flattered by the names to which he is to be distinguished." The baby had been named George Bingham Rollins. He also asked that Mrs. Rollins send Eliza "the size of the new inhabitant's head in order that she may send him a fancy hat."

The same letter has the first hint of dissatisfaction with the

Art-Union. "I have discovered since I have been here that the present managers of the Art Union display in some cases gross favoritism in the purchase of their pictures."

In New York Bingham began work on *The Emigration of Daniel Boone,* or *Daniel Boone Escorting Settlers thru the Cumberland Gap* as it is also called. Here, then, is yet another intertwining of George's life with that of the great folk hero.

"Old Dan'l Boone in a buckskin with a gun at his side" was George's first effort at a figure, a sign for a tavern. He planned a political poster for Boone County of "Daniel Boone in a death struggle with an Indian." The death of Daniel Boone was well within Bingham's memory, and the old man's adventures were told over and over so that a growing youngster would always recall them. Boonville, Boone County, Boon's Lick, were all reminders. Bingham had every reason to think that he had chosen a popular subject. He thought that he might sell the picture to one of the art unions, or perhaps finance the engraving himself and reap the whole profit.

On April 14, 1851, the American Art-Union received the finished picture, but declined to buy it. They had accepted another picture on the same subject by another artist. Bingham then arranged to have Goupil and Company of Paris make a steel engraving. He sold them the copyright, the first they had ever bought from an American painter, but by agreement, Bingham kept the original painting.

The work was done in Paris, but Bingham was disappointed by the results. Instead of a steel engraving, a lithograph was made. A lithograph is made on a stone surface, not a steel plate. (The mix-up came about through a verbal agreement with Goupil's agent in New York.) However, the lithographs sold, and some of them are still around to be seen today.

A comparison of one of the lithographs with the original painting, now owned by Washington University in St. Louis, indicates that once Bingham got the picture back from Paris he did considerable repainting. Some figures have been painted out; the rocky cliffs have narrowed; the storm clouds are darker.

Whatever the merits of the first version or the second one, whether the picture is genre or historical, the painting caught

Daniel Boone Escorting Settlers thru the Cumberland Gap, 1851–52 *Courtesy of Collection, Washington University, St. Louis*

a moment of time in the life of this country. Boone is in the lead. He wears a yellow homespun outfit and over his left shoulder is a long rifle. His expression is calm, fearless, and he looks every inch the leader of men that in truth he was. His hand holds the reins of a white horse that carries his wife, Rebecca. Her face, too, is calm and serene. She and their daughter, Jemima, who is slightly behind her, are the apex of the pyramid. These two, according to Marshall's *History of Kentucky,* were the first white women in the state. Bingham recognized their bravery by dedicating the Goupil lithograph to "The Mothers and Daughters of the West."

At Boone's left is Flanders Callaway, Jemima's husband. Callaway wears the coonskin cap often associated with the pioneers, and he also has a long rifle. On the right a young man hesitates in the march to tie the strings of his moccasins. In front of the party is a lemon and white pointer.

The sky in the painting is lighted by a brilliant shaft of sunlight that breaks through the dark clouds and adds drama to the scene. The picture scarcely needs a title. Looking at it is enough to know that here are men and women setting out to make new homes in a new, an unknown land.

Mary Amend Bingham, George's mother, died on January 27, 1851. She was sixty-one. Her lifetime took in many changes. She had gone West with her husband, her father, and her children. She had borne children and buried them; she had lost her father, "a soldier of the Revolution." She had lost her husband at a time when his life had showed great promise. Alone, she had brought up her children and she saw them become good, able men and women. One became famous, but she loved them all. In her life as a teacher she touched the lives of many students and passed on to them the love of learning she had herself found in a small boarding school in the Blue Ridge Mountains. Mary Amend Bingham could well be pointed out as one of those "Mothers and Daughters of the West," to whom her son dedicated the lithograph of the *Emigration of Daniel Boone*.

She is buried in the cemetery in Arrow Rock. In the same plot rests Henry Vest, Jr.'s wife and three little girls who died of cholera. Tradition is strong in the family, and in the town, that Elizabeth Bingham and the baby, Joseph are also buried there. The cemetery records do not give their names, and the old, old gravestones are so covered with lichens as to be unreadable. As Elizabeth's death occurred in Arrow Rock, it seems reasonable to accept the tradition.

Today a giant maple tree has grown up to shade the entire family plot. It is a quiet, peaceful cemetery. At sunset birds fly over, back to their nests by the river. Time seems to stand still— yesterday merges into today. A sense of the presence of George Caleb Bingham can come to one who stands by the gravestones of his beloved family as the breeze comes and goes in the branches of the maple tree.

Sketch No. 87
Courtesy, St. Louis Mercantile Library

The Election Series

The year that began with the death of his mother was also the year in which Bingham went ahead in what was to be one of his finest achievements—the painting of the genre pictures known as the Election Series.

On this series and on the more than twenty river pictures rest the fame of the artist. It is a solid foundation. The existing Election Series is four paintings with a unifying subject; they were painted between 1851–1855. Bingham in his early forties was at the height of his powers.

A not so happy development marred the early part of this period in the artist's final open break with the Art-Union. This took place in 1852, although there are earlier rumblings in his letters to Major Rollins.

An article in the December 1851 *Bulletin* seriously offended Bingham. The gist of it was that William S. Mount was "the only one of our figure painters who has thoroughly succeeded in delineating American life. Bingham has made some good studies of western character, but so entirely undisciplined yet mannered and often mean in subject . . . want of earnestness . . . repetitions . . . [he is] hardly entitled to rank." The article was signed with only the initial "W."

Bingham was furious! He demanded from Colonel Warner, secretary of the Art-Union, space in the *Bulletin* to make reply. Warner disclaimed writing the article and assured Bingham he could have space in the big April issue.

By April Bingham had brooded too long over the insult to his work. He wrote Warner that he no longer wanted space in the *Bulletin,* and that he had decided to sue the Art-Union for "the attack on my works, so uncalled for, unprovoked, and unsustained by the slightest evidence." He had already hired a New York lawyer.

Nothing came of the lawsuit. The Art-Union, already in financial trouble, was dissolved, and there was no one left to sue. A good and rewarding association, on both sides, ended on an unhappy, hostile note.

Canvassing for a Vote, County Election, Stump Speaking, Verdict of the People, are the titles of the paintings which are now in the Election Series. Two lost paintings, *Stump Orator* and *Country Politician,* should also be included; perhaps one day they will be found. Only to read the titles can bring out the spirit of the time and the place Bingham was portraying. The vitality he put into the paintings is amazing.

All four of the existing Election Series now hang in public places. This is an advantage not to be overlooked. Many Bingham paintings are privately owned. No one can expect the owners to throw open their doors and say to the world, "Come in." But the Election Series *is* available in St. Louis and in Kansas City, Missouri.

From any politician's point of view—and Bingham was a prime example of the saying, "Man is a political animal"— the first thing a candidate must do is get out and meet the voters. In the 1850s it was much harder than it is now. No radio or TV had been invented, and even newspapers had sparse circulation. A good party man got some help in the political conventions for which Bingham painted banners, but personal contact was the surest way to get the votes "from the forks of the creek."

In *Canvassing for a Vote,* the candidate is doing this necessary piece of work (Color Plate VII). Three men sit outside a tavern, probably the one at Arrow Rock; a fourth stands behind them, and a fifth, barely visible, peers in at the tavern window. The composition is in the form of a triangle with one long, sloping side. That long line is the candidate, persuading, appealing, pleading for the promise of votes. His face shows his conviction that he is the *right man for the office.* A point of light touches his upraised forefinger as he tries to hold his listeners' interest.

Each voter listens in his own way. The portly man with the long-stemmed clay pipe is smiling, but this may mean only that he looks forward to a good supper or a dram of whiskey in the tavern. Sprawled in a chair is a prosperous farmer who looks as if he might say at any moment, "I'm from Missouri. You've got to show me." The man with the fringe of black beard, standing behind the others, has a question to ask the minute the candidate stops for breath.

Light streams into the picture from a towering cloud bank. All the men are dressed in lively colors and have ruddy out-of-doors complexions. To find them the candidate must have taken to the campaign trail. Bingham had done this himself, and he passes his knowledge on to those who look at the painting.

First mention of *Canvassing for a Vote* is in a letter to Major Rollins. Bingham was planning such a picture for Goupil and Company to make a lithograph. Evidently the artist was now convinced that lithography was a coming thing. But once the details were settled, Bingham had to write to Goupil that the picture would not be ready as soon as he had promised. His portrait work was unusually heavy, and he had started another political genre painting.

At last the picture was finished and dated 1852. It was shipped to Paris for the lithographer to do his work. In 1853 the lithograph was published. But where was the original painting?

A hundred and two years went by before that question could be answered. In 1954 a doctor living in Florida offered *Canvassing for a Vote* for sale to the William Rockhill Nelson Gallery of Art in Kansas City. The doctor had received it as a gift ten years before. His reason for selling was an excellent one. "I think it is too valuable to have in a house where a number of children are playing."

The director of the William Rockhill Nelson Gallery was convinced that the picture was a genuine Bingham, and that it was part of the Election Series. The gallery bought the picture. After a hundred years, it was in immediate need of restoration.

The painstaking process of restoring an oil painting is unknown to most people. Winifred Shields in the Kansas City *Star* of October 31, 1954, describes this particular restoration.

When the painting arrived here it was routed to James Roth's studio on the second floor of the gallery where a delicate operation was performed. The canvas was found to be rotted and warped and the paint brittle and cracked was nearing the stage where it would soon peel off.

The surface of the painting was faced with paper and ironed into a pad of wax. Working from the back of the picture, Roth completely removed the old worn canvas and put in its place a brand new one. Through this tricky maneuver the paint itself was never disturbed.

The political painting that had delayed the finishing of *Canvassing for a Vote* was *County Election*. For a politician the logical next step after talking to the voters is the election. Bingham knew his ground. (Color Plate VIII)

As the idea for *County Election* grew in his mind, for that is where all pictures start, it took over the artist completely. Ideas boiled up; plans were made and discarded, and remade. *County Election* was his occupation "constantly for three months," reported the state newspapers. The picture became a source of pride and of *curiosity*. What would it be like, and who would be in the picture?

The planning took the longest time. It was a difficult subject. The canvas was three by four feet. At least sixty figures were to be painted on it. How to keep the light and dark in balance—how to bring out the important and play down the lesser details? The artist struggled with the answers.

In his lost painting, *The Stump Orator,* Bingham had been roundly, soundly criticized in the *Literary World*. That was five years ago, but sensitive as he was, Bingham no doubt remembered every word. ". . . makes one's eyes ache to look at it . . . the eye is distracted and carried all over the canvas without a resting place . . . in color it is unmistakably bad. . . ." He was determined that no such things could be said of *County Election*.

The ballot in Missouri was not a secret one at the time Bingham was working on his ambitious painting. The voter announced his choices to the judge of the election, and they were recorded by the clerk. A man could vote in any township in a county, though he must swear that he had voted only once and would vote no more. Workers for candidates, called "strikers," went with the voter right up to the judge and the clerk. Elections took three days.

The weather being fine, voting in *County Election* was done on the courthouse steps of a small western town. On the top step is the judge, the high point of interest in the picture. He is "a thick pursy-looking citizen," said the *Missouri Statesman*, "engaged in swearing a voter, a well-set Irishman in a red flannel shirt."

Down the steps to the left are the crowding citizens, plus the ever-present dog. Some men are talking together, some are drinking at a "cake and liquor stand." (The latter was probably for the sale of gingerbread and hard cider. And do not underestimate the alcoholic content of hard cider!) One of the voters is "falling down drunk"; he is being lugged to the voting place by a determined "striker."

In the right-hand corner, another voter has also drunk not wisely but too well; he sits with his head wrapped in a ragged bandage. Two boys are on the ground playing mumble-the-peg. The boy with the round straw hat is Horace Bingham.

With sure skill the artist leads our eyes down the main street of the little town. Stores, some homes, and the slender spire of a church are there. From far off, a man on horseback is hurrying to the voting. The tall slim trees recall the many engravings of the Renaissance masters that Bingham used to copy, and details of the architecture of the buildings is somewhat like theirs, too.

Enthusiasm for the picture spread throughout the state. Major Rollins was especially pleased. He saw it not as a Missouri picture, but as a national one. Such a scene, he wrote, could be met with "on the Arrostock in Maine, or in the City of New York, or on the Rio Grande in Texas."

At the urging of friends Bingham wrote to Goupil about making an engraving. Before an agreement could be reached, the artist changed his hat again and became a politician. He was elected a delegate to the Whig National Convention, meeting in Baltimore in June 1852. He took *County Election* with him and opened a subscription book for those who wished to order engravings.

As Philadelphia is near Baltimore, Bingham went there to talk to engravers. He met John Sartain, one of the best American engravers, liked him, and decided that he should have the contract for engraving *County Election*.

Bingham wanted to finance the deal on his own, but being in need of cash he wrote at once to Major Rollins. Sartain's price was low, twelve hundred dollars. Bingham asked for a loan of that amount and offered a mortgage on his Arrow Rock property as security. In a postscript he cautioned Rollins not to mention the price as Sartain regularly charged four thousand dollars for such work, but he "will engage upon mine as a work of love."

Major Rollins at once sent the money, as he had done before and as he would do again. Such friends are rare indeed!

Now Bingham decided to make a tour of the country getting subscriptions for the engravings. But Sartain needed the original to make the plates. To solve the problem Bingham painted, quickly, another *County Election,* and set forth on tour.

Also with him was *The Emigration of Daniel Boone* which had not yet been sold. Two towns in western Missouri on his route were Columbia and Glasgow. By Christmas he was in St. Louis, but he had to stop his tour and catch up on the portrait painting. As soon as possible he left for New Orleans, carrying *County Election* (2). Subscriptions sold well. The picture was exhibited in a store and seen there by Robert J. Ward of Louisville, Kentucky, who wanted to buy it.

This was a stroke of good luck! Bingham priced the picture at twelve hundred dollars, the amount of the Arrow Rock mortgage. He also had an agreement with Mr. Ward that he might keep the picture to finish his tour.

This part of his trip carried him through Kentucky and the picture was successful in attracting subscribers and attention. He wrote to Major Rollins, ". . . the press was profuse in its commendations, and without a dissenting voice."

There was, however, one "dissenting voice." An irate subscriber wrote to the Lexington, Kentucky, newspaper that the picture "is not only a slander . . . but places weapons in the hands of the enemies of the Republic." Bingham may never have seen the letter, but it did him no harm. Over a hundred subscriptions were sold in Lexington.

During his stay in Philadelphia, Bingham was joined by Eliza and Clara. It may have been on this stay that a family story about Bingham's absentmindedness took place.

"Once while living in one of Philadelphia's famous 'row houses' he entered what he thought was his own house and proceeded to the living room, absorbed in thought. He happened to glance up at a picture over the mantel, and realized *it was not his picture,* and he was in the wrong house. Much chagrinned, he managed to escape without anyone in the house knowing."

During November Bingham wrote to his friend: "As your knowledge of my habits may lead you to suppose, I have not been idle during my sojourn here. I am very busily engaged on my companion to *County Election*—the *County Canvass.* . . . As much as you admired the *County Election,* I think you will be still better pleased with the present work."

County Canvass is known today by the title *Stump Speaking.*

Work went fast on this new picture. Bingham knew his way now, and he kept at his work with skill and imagination. Another letter to Major Rollins has a ring of triumph in it. "I am getting along fully up to my expectations . . . I should like much for you to see it [*Stump Speaking*] in its present state. I do not think you would counsel any change in the design, and if you did I scarcely think your advice would be followed."

Later he wrote that the picture was becoming much larger than he had planned. "A new head is continually popping up and demanding a place . . . instead of the select company which my plan first embraced, I have an audience that would be no discredit to the most populous precinct of Buncombe."

He located the picture "in the vicinity of a mill (Kit Bullard's, perhaps.)" The cider barrel having been used earlier, he was placing "in the back ground a watermellon waggon." The orator he describes as a wiry politician "grown gray in the pursuit of office and the service of the party . . . but I have placed behind him a shrewd, clear-headed opponent who is busy taking notes."

In the inevitable "key" that each of these many-figured pictures called forth, the "clear-headed opponent" was said to represent Bingham himself; the orator was supposed to be Darwin Sappington. The very fat man behind the orator was generally considered to be Meredith Miles Marmaduke, former governor. "Marmaduke was so insulted," C. B. Rollins wrote, "when even his friends recognized him as this figure that he threatened a libel suit and went so far as to challenge Bingham to a duel."

Bingham always denied these identifications.

On April 14, 1854, Bingham signed an agreement with Goupil for the engraving of *Stump Speaking*. Sartain *still* had not finished engraving *County Election*. For *Stump Speaking*

Stump Speaking, 1854 *Courtesy of Collection of the Boatmen's National Bank of St. Louis*

Bingham said that he had "terms as favorable as any artist ever obtained from a publisher."

There were to be four classes of prints. First were Artist's Proofs. These were the first fifty to be made from the engraver's plates. They sold for forty dollars each. Of this Bingham got twelve dollars. Next came Proofs Before Letters (without title). Fifty of these sold for twenty dollars each; Bingham to get six dollars. The third class was hand-colored prints. The price was to be set by the publisher, with Bingham getting five dollars each. The last class was the plain print, ten dollars; Bingham to get three dollars. The painting was to be the property of the artist, unless it was sold for a price of two thousand dollars.

Bingham had had a difficult apprenticeship, but now he had arrived. He wrote to Major Rollins about how he felt. "The fact is that I am getting to be quite conceited, whispering sometimes to myself, that in the familiar line which I have chosen, I am the greatest among all the disciples of the brush which my native land has yet produced. When I get this picture completed and published, in conjunction with *County Election,* I think I shall have laid the foundation of a fortune sufficient to meet my humble expectations, and place my little family beyond the reach of want, should I be taken away from them."

He was already planning his next painting, *Verdict of the People.* It was, he wrote, "to cap the clymax." He wanted to paint the end of a close political contest as the judge announced the results of the election. It was a scene he himself knew well.

He started working on it in Philadelphia in the late spring of 1854. By September the *Philadelphia Register* was commenting on "the infinite variety" of the artist.

Always concerned with national politics, Bingham wrote to Major Rollins that he feared he would no longer be regarded as a Whig in Missouri. He could not agree with the support the Missouri Whigs in Congress gave to the Kansas-Nebraska Act. When the vote was taken, not only every Whig from Missouri, but every other member of the state's delegation except Thomas Hart Benton voted in favor of the bill. The act left the question of slavery up to the vote of the settlers in these two territories. Bingham saw it as a grave mistake. He wrote: "The deed is done, and a storm is now brewing in the north which will sweep onward with a fury which no human force can with-stand."

Back in Independence, Missouri, Bingham jogged the memory of some slow-paying customers, and painted a few portraits to make expenses. Once again his letters were filled with much anxiety over the division of the North and the South. In June he told Major Rollins he had taken *Verdict of the People* to Goupil's New York office. In a later letter he wrote with fatherly pride, "Do you not think our daughter Clara is becoming something fit to be bragged about. . . ."

Bingham and Goupil did not at this time reach an agree-ment on the terms for engraving *Verdict of the People*. When the painting was returned to the artist, he took it to Columbia, Jefferson City, and St. Louis for short exhibitions. There was not much time for he wanted to take the picture with him when he made his long-planned trip to Paris.

Paris was a part of the dream of every American painter. The French capital was the art capital of the world. Its Salon, ruled by the Royal Academy of Painting and Sculpture, was all-powerful. Earlier young artists had revolted against its reac-tionary policies, but still—Paris was the place for an artist.

Bingham had achieved success in many ways, but there was criticism of his work in some quarters as "untutored." His taste in choosing genre subjects was called into question. By go-ing to Paris he would have access to the great world of art—a world undreamed of by the rivermen, the trappers, the strug-gling politicians of the little western towns. He was now forty-four years old, and he knew that he must go soon, or not at all. As he had once started out, stubbornly, to walk to St. Louis, so now George Caleb Bingham gathered together all his resources and took his chance—he was going to Paris.

Verdict of the People, which he was taking along in order to make contact with an engraver, was another of the many-figured Election Series. Again the crowd of voters and officials is massed against the town courthouse. The judge stands on the top step to read the election results aloud. He is dressed in white, the better to emphasize his importance. An American flag with thirty-one stars in 1854 hangs over the crowd. On a balcony some ladies look down on the scene, recalling the "fair virtuous Whig ladies" of 1844 in Boonville. A hat peddler wearing a stack of hats on his head sells his wares around the town pump. One voter uses the top of his beaver hat as a desk to write on; maybe he is a reporter taking notes. The boys, the dogs, the drunks are all there, plus a juicy red watermelon just split open.

Figures in *Verdict of the People* are larger than those in the other crowd scenes. This allows for more detail. The planning and placing of the people in the crowd is masterful. Bingham learned his lessons well.

The plan to reproduce *Verdict of the People* as a lithograph ran into a strange twist of fate. Bingham finally sent a photograph to Goupil in Paris as late as 1869. The stone for a lithograph was made from this, and two prints were pulled. C. B. Rollins recalled the night his father and Bingham sat in the library at La Grange and examined the prints. Bingham sent an order for "a large number" to Paris. Before the order could be carried out, the Franco-Prussian War broke out. Goupil's establishment was destroyed; the lithographic stone was broken. Only the two prints survived.

From 1851 to 1855 is a short time for an artist to produce works of the magnitude of the Election Series. But this was by no means all that was done by Bingham in this period. He made other genre paintings and many portraits.

The Trapper's Return, a genre painting of 1851, is much like *Fur Traders Descending the Missouri.* There is the old trader, his half-Indian son, the pirogue, and even the "small black animal." But in a mysterious way some of the charm of the first picture seems lost. The misty look of the water has changed; the snags are gone; the shore is no longer a dream but a jutting reality. The "small black animal" stands on four legs, and there is no mystery about him now. He *is* a bear cub. The Detroit Institute of Art owns the picture. From the list of cities outside the United States where it has been shown— Munich, Hamburg, Berlin, Düsseldorf, Rome, and Milan— *Trapper's Return* may be the most traveled of all Bingham's work.

12

Sketch No. 33
Courtesy, St. Louis Mercantile Library

A Missouri Artist in Europe

The plan to go to Paris in 1855 was postponed until the following summer. Bingham, like most other people, had to be practical in making his financial arrangements. He painted long and hard to get together money for the trip and to keep his family in comfort while they were abroad.

It was toward the last of June, 1856, that he arrived in Boston. He carried with him a commission from the state of Missouri for two full-length portraits of George Washington and Thomas Jefferson, to be displayed in the capitol building at Jefferson City. Major Rollins' efforts brought this opportunity to his friend. Payment was to be thirty-five hundred dollars.

As a preliminary to painting the portraits, Bingham set about copying the famous Gilbert Stuart paintings of the two early American statesmen. He also made a copy of Stuart's portrait of Martha Washington.

There were other private commissions in Boston "to the amount of four hundred dollars." In Philadelphia a leading picture dealer liked Bingham's copies so well that he ordered six more of them. "He pays for these copies $380.00. I painted them in less than two weeks time. I have also painted other pictures for different individuals to the amount of $300.00."

With this kind of financial stability Bingham was ready for his first trip abroad. The steamship *Vigo* sailed from the port of New York City, bound for France and the port of Havre, August 14, 1856. Aboard her was George Caleb Bingham, his wife, Eliza, and his daughter, Clara, who was eleven years old. Horace, fifteen, stayed in school in the United States, joining the family later.

Of the journey Bingham wrote, "The voyage was much more agreeable than I expected to find it . . . [a] severe gale four days out of New York lasted sixteen hours. During [it] we suffered much from sea-sickness. As soon as the violence of the winds subsided we became ourselves, and could do ample justice to the abundant fare spread before us."

At that time an Atlantic crossing took about two weeks. On September first the Binghams arrived in Paris. Goupil and Company sent a young man to help them find a place to live. They made the unpleasant discovery that there were no boardinghouses in Paris, such as Mrs. Brawner's in Washington.

For a parlor and two small bedrooms they were obliged to pay thirty dollars a month. Meals would come to about twenty-five dollars. And to this must be added thirteen dollars a month for a studio large enough for Bingham to work on the Washington and Jefferson canvases. He wrote these gloomy details to Major Rollins. University of Missouri students in Columbia were then paying from two to two and a half dollars per week for board, lodging, washing, fuel, and light. The contrast was dismaying.

But the beauty of Paris, the magnificent architecture, and his first visits to the Louvre delighted the artist. Now he walked through the galleries and saw the originals from which the steel engravings had been made, the ones he had copied with "lead pencil upon paper," such a long time ago.

After the first excitement wore off, "the great collection of works of Art there from all nations and all schools" seemed overpowering, even confusing. Recalling the days when he had thought of being a lawyer, Bingham wrote that a visitor to the Louvre could be "like a juror bewildered by a mass of conflicting testimony. . . .

"I shall be compelled to visit the great gallery often before I can be able properly to appreciate the treasure which it contains," he concluded.

Soon an uncomfortable financial pinch began to distract him. Paris was a costly place to live! He had budgeted a hundred dollars a month for the three of them. Was that going to be enough? And the city was so big, and hard for a stranger to make his way around. The language barrier tripped him at every turn. Why he had not tried to learn a little French before coming to Paris is never explained. Later he insisted that Horace and Clara learn both French and German.

The studio that he had rented was not satisfactory. When he wanted changes made, he was certain he was being cheated. In these times of frustration Bingham would go to one of the reading rooms where for a small fee he could read the New York papers.

Such reading, however, was not likely to make a devoted Union man feel any better. Political affairs were fast growing worse. Back in Louisville, in early June, Bingham had written to Major Rollins, "Slavery is doomed. . . . I myself have gone clear over to the Black Republicans . . . although in Missouri I might support the American Party."

From Paris he wrote in reference to the national situation, "I hope that good may come out of this evil—that Frémont may be elected." John Charles Frémont, son-in-law of Thomas Hart Benton, was the first Presidential nominee of the new Republican party.

Early in Bingham's stay in Paris he went to call at the American Embassy. James Young Mason was the United States ambassador, a man of strong southern sympathies. When he learned that Bingham was from Missouri he assumed that the artist would agree with his political views. It was a mistake he would not make again! Bingham wrote to Rollins, "As there was no cudgel over my head, or mob to apply tar and feathers I felt at liberty to return thrust for thrust . . . in the course of half an hour [he was] quite willing to drop the subject."

After two months in Paris Bingham moved himself and his family to Düsseldorf, Germany. This old fortified Prussian city was on the banks of the Rhine. It was a famous center of nineteenth-century German romantic painting. Wilhelm von Schadow-Godenhaus, founder of the Düsseldorf school of art, was living when Bingham went there, although there is no reason to think that the Missourian was a student in any formal sense.

The influence of the Düsseldorf school had once been strong. Its founder was said to have "educated a generation of painters." By the time Bingham got there the Düsseldorf school had started to decline. But his enthusiasm for the city, the artists he met, and the style of life he shared runs through his letters sent back to Missouri. "I question much if there can be found a city in the world where an artist who sincerely worships Truth and Nature can find a more congenial atmosphere, or obtain more ready facilities in the prosecution of his studies . . ."

The city was a small one: thirty to forty thousand people, and five hundred of these were practicing artists. Principal show-places were the thirteenth-century Church of St. Lambertus, the Italian-style Church of St. Andreas, the City Hall built in 1570, and the equestrian statue of Count Palatine John William by Grupello. Although Bingham knew no more German than he did French, he found it far easier to get around than in Paris.

Of the five hundred artists in Düsseldorf, six were from the United States. One of these was Henry Lewis; Bingham had known him in St. Louis. But his most fortunate contact, made the third day he was in Düsseldorf, was in meeting Emanuel Leutze.

Leutze was the painter of the famous *Washington Crossing the Delaware,* known to generations of American school children. With warm hospitality he welcomed the newcomer and at once helped him to find a suitable place to live—No. 35 Kaiser Strasse—and he also helped locate a studio. Leutze was born in Germany, but had come to the United States as a child, and he spoke both English and German. His friendly help was in-valuable.

The Binghams settled into their apartment; they made friends; they entertained. Clara and Horace, who had joined the family, were in school and becoming good at speaking German, as was Eliza. "I do not make any progress with the German lan-guage," Bingham admitted, "being entirely preoccupied with pictures."

A story preserved by his family is that in Düsseldorf Bing-ham always carried a sketchbook if he went out to shop. If he could not make the shopkeeper understand him, he would draw a quick sketch, which worked very well.

Bingham finished first the portrait of George Washington. Then before he began on the Jefferson portrait, he painted an-other version of his popular genre picture, *Jolly Flatboatmen in Port*. It had been ten years since he made the first picture, but the third version is still lively and filled with the joy of life on the river.

Once again the crew watches as one of their number dances. In this picture there are more onlookers than in the others. Twenty-one can be counted. Two men on the far right in their sober business suits are intent on the cargo, not the dance.

A woman is tucked into this all-male world. She leans over some bit of cargo, and her young son is beside her. A black man holding one of the big oars keeps the flatboat away from the dock. The port is St. Louis, a spot so well known to Bingham that he could paint it in far-away Düsseldorf with complete fidelity.

Of all three flatboat pictures, Bingham was regularly asked why he had not included a dog. He always answered that the dog was there, "but in the hold."

Bingham tried his hand at painting another river during his stay in Germany. He painted a castle high on a hill overlooking the Rhine. It was called *Moonlight Scene.*

In November, Bingham's hope for Frémont as President was dashed. James Buchanan, Democrat, was elected in 1856. Also, the artist's hope that Horace would get an appointment to West Point had to be put aside.

Düsseldorf was famous for its carnival. As Lent approached, Bingham wrote, "Mask balls, mask procession, and every conceivable species of tom-foolery becomes respectable. . . . I am becoming rather too old to relish such sport, [but] I accompanied Eliza and Clara to one of the balls." As it was to be a masked ball he sent Horace out to buy his mask, asking only that it have a Roman nose. Horace came back with the mask. Here, in his letter to Major Rollins, Bingham drew a small sketch of a devil's mask. So attired, he took the ladies to the ball. In spite of thinking he was "rather too old," he enjoyed himself, and wrote to Columbia about his successes.

"While I wore the mask every person with whom I came in contact took me cordially by the hand and seemed to recognize an old acquaintance, and I could not but feel mortified when, throwing it off, I found myself alone and unnoticed."

The two large portraits ordered by the state of Missouri were finished. Bingham had received many favorable comments from Americans who dropped in at his Düsseldorf studio. But that was not enough. He wanted to take them to Missouri himself. He wanted to see them hanging in the capitol. Possibly he had the more practical reason that he might receive other commissions if he went, but the satisfaction he sought was reason enough.

The Washington canvas was 144 inches by 96 inches. No size is known on the Jefferson canvas, but it was probably about the same. Bingham had had the advantage in painting Jefferson of talking with Jefferson's "old and intimate friend, ex-Governor Coles" (Illinois Territory). Coles had Bingham to stay at his home in Boston while he copied the Gilbert Stuart head. From Coles he learned that Jefferson often draped himself in a long reddish-brown coat, "reaching almost to his ancles." He also wore his own invention, "the Jefferson shoe."

After the paintings were complete, there developed a struggle over the framing. Bingham thought the state should pay for the frames; the officials in charge thought Bingham should supply frames. As these were very large frames, it was a matter of considerable money. Letters went back and forth across the ocean. Inevitably Major Rollins was drawn into the controversy. Inevitably, also, Bingham lost his temper with the officials.

Finally, in order to break the deadlock, Bingham had frames made in Düsseldorf at the cost of seventy-one dollars each. This, he wrote, was about half what they would have cost in St. Louis. He then booked passage on a steamship to deliver the pictures. "My entire expense to Düsseldorf and back is not more than $250," he explained to Major Rollins.

Across the bleak Atlantic in the icy month of January 1859 went the artist and his pictures. On reaching Jefferson City he found that the frame of the Washington portrait was badly damaged. It had to be repaired in St. Louis. The portraits were not presented to the General Assembly until February.

When they were put on view, the portrait of Jefferson in the lower chamber, the portrait of Washington in the Senate chamber, the praise was lavish. Perhaps the general good feeling and the excellence of the paintings softened the officials. A bill was quickly passed to pay Bingham for the frames and the customs charges—$320.

On March twelfth the artist came back to the General Assembly with a surprise gift. It was a portrait done in needlework, with silk floss, a bust of George Washington. Bingham's daughter, fourteen-year-old Clara, had made it. The needlework was so good that "at a short distance" it resembled an oil painting. The legislators responded gallantly and voted that the gift be hung above the Speaker's chair.

While Bingham was in Jefferson City, the legislators commissioned him to paint two more of the great men of the nation: Andrew Jackson and Henry Clay. The price was to be the same as for the first two—thirty-five hundred dollars. Again Major Rollins guided this commission through the legislative body.

But the melancholy truth is that none of these portraits survived the fire that destroyed the Missouri capitol in 1911. Seven Bingham portraits were lost in that fire; eleven had earlier been lost when the University of Missouri burned in 1892.

After leaving Jefferson City, and visiting in Columbia, Bingham went on to Kansas City.*

In Kansas City Bingham painted one of the finest of all his portraits. The subject was Dr. Benoist Troost, the first physician in the city. Dr. Troost was born in Holland. He was about seventy-five when Bingham painted him, a big, hearty man with an air of authority about him. The portrait shows him in his library, his finger holding his place in a leather-bound book; he has just glanced up from his reading, and his bright blue eyes are knowledgeable and searching.

The companion portrait of Mrs. Troost, born Mary Gillis of a pioneer family, does not compare with that of her husband. It is competent and may have been a good likeness but the excellence that sets Dr. Troost's portrait apart was not duplicated.

"Humboldt was one of those wonders of the world, like Aristotle, like Julius Caesar . . . ," wrote Ralph Waldo Emerson

---

* For the purpose of keeping geography clear, Kansas City in this book is always Kansas City, *Missouri*. There is occasional confusion because of the names with Kansas City, *Kansas*. In Bingham's time Kansas City, Kansas, was a small town with the name of Wyandotte. It is now a thriving city located across the state line from Kansas City, Missouri.

Doctor Benoist Troost, 1859 *Courtesy of Nelson Gallery—Atkins Museum, Kansas City, Missouri* (Gift of the Kansas City Board of Education)

of the famous German scientist, Baron Alexander von Humboldt. He was astronomer, geographer, geophysicist, botanist, explorer—and on and on. He was revered in his own country, and also in the United States where he traveled. The city of St. Louis with its large German population decided to honor him, and the Mercantile Library Board of Direction called for Bingham to paint his portrait.

Humboldt was ninety at the time, and by sad coincidence he died the very day the agreement between the Mercantile Library and the artist was reached. Bingham assured the board that he would go to Berlin and do his work from photographs.

As soon as Bingham got back to Germany, he went to Berlin. He painted the old scientist in his library where he had spent most of his last years. The snowy white hair and the snowy white neckcloth were highlights of a very successful portrait. After setting up his background in Berlin, Bingham took the Humboldt picture back to Düsseldorf. There he was also working on the Clay and Jackson portraits.

Bingham's pleasant life in Düsseldorf was resumed. He was thinking of taking a trip into Italy. He and Eliza considered placing Horace and Clara in a school in Belgium to improve their French. The family had been in Germany about three years. Suddenly the death of Eliza's father, Dr. Robert Thomas, called them back to the United States.

Art critics have thought that Bingham's work was not improved by his stay in Düsseldorf. The school of art there was known for its literary qualities, its attention to details, and for the hard polished surface of its pictures. Bingham was not a student when he arrived, but he did admire the work of other artists of the Düsseldorf school, and he acquired some of the "finish" they used. The result was to damage the freshness that was one of his most admirable qualities. With some notable exceptions, the quality of the pictures Bingham painted after his return from Germany declined.

Established once more in Columbia, Missouri, Bingham's work on the Humboldt portrait and the Clay and Jackson commissions continued. He went to Washington, D.C., to study the Sully painting of the head of Jackson, as he had earlier studied the Stuart heads of Washington and Jefferson. In April of 1860 he took the Humboldt portrait to St. Louis.

Andrew Jackson's portrait was to show the general on horseback. Bingham went to some lengths to make it realistic. He wrote Major Rollins on September fifth, "The window of my studio commands the main avenue leading from Kansas City toward New Mexico through which thousands of horses, oxen, and mules are almost daily passing, and I have been thus able to make the Charger of the Old Hero as near perfect as possible."

Not everyone agreed with him on the finished picture!

13

Sketch No. 70
Courtesy, St. Louis Mercantile Library

Bingham Joins the Union Army

During the months that he was working on the Humboldt portrait in Columbia, Bingham took some time to stay with his friend Major Rollins at La Grange, a few miles from town. It was a delightful springtime in the Missouri countryside. A story of the visit, one of many, has been told by C. B. Rollins.

I remember first seeing Bingham about 1860 . . . The time I first recall him he arrived one evening for a visit, and I, a youngster, was deputed to show him to his room. Filled with my own importance, I walked briskly ahead, carrying a candle to light the way, while Bingham followed with his valise and portfolio. I set the candle down, and then with childish curiosity lingered to see what the portfolio, which he had begun to unstrap, might contain.

He laid out a few things and I recall my disappointment at the meager contents. But my curiosity was yet to be satisfied in full measure. After unpacking his artist's materials, he took off his coat and hung it on a chair, went to the bureau, untied and removed his choker, and then to my unspeakable amazement, lifted off the entire top of his head, exposing a great white dome. I was speechless with fright and I fled with terror; I had never seen or heard of a wig.

My mother finally quieted my fears by explaining to me that when Mr. Bingham was about nineteen years old he had a severe attack of measles which left him bald . . . From that hour, Mr. Bingham assumed great importance in my eyes; for *me* he was a marked man.

Mr. Rollins continues in "Some Recollections of George Caleb Bingham," published in the *Missouri Historical Review,* to tell how he and the other children in the family looked forward to the artist's visits. Bingham loved children, and would tell them stories and illustrate the stories with sketches of the characters. "Some of these sketches I still have," Rollins wrote.

Kansas City, Independence, and Lexington, Missouri, are not far apart. Bingham could have worked on portraits in these towns, and others nearby, as he gathered details for the portrait of Andrew Jackson.

Judge Samuel Locke Sawyer, "generally regarded as one of the most eminent lawyers of western Missouri," was painted when he lived in Lexington. Later he moved to Independence where the portrait now hangs in the century-old home of his great-grandson and namesake.

Claiborne Fox Jackson, elected governor of Missouri in 1861, found time that year to pose for Bingham. A strong supporter of the South, he served only seven months when the state convention of 1861 replaced him with Hamilton Gamble. Jackson continued to regard himself as head of the "government of Missouri in exile," until his death in 1862. Bingham's portrait of "Old Claib" as he called the governor is another example of the many, many men and women who made history in the state who were put on canvas by the artist.

The next few months were to be the last of peace in the United States for four long bitter years. The Civil War was even longer in the border country of Missouri and Kansas where violence had broken out as early as the 1850s. The prophecy Bingham had made was about to be realized, for "the storm brewing in the north" was upon the country.

Tension in Missouri was high. Bingham refused to moderate his views. Indeed, he was *unable* to compromise. "His opinions were his convictions," C. B. Rollins said. "I am for man conditionally, though for the Union unconditionally" was a statement by Bingham that was widely quoted.

January eighth was the anniversary of Andrew Jackson's famous victory at the Battle of New Orleans in 1815. On that day Bingham chose to deliver to the General Assembly in Jefferson City the portraits of Andrew Jackson and Henry Clay. As he walked into the capitol a thirty-three gun salute roared forth, honoring Jackson, and rattling the windows of all Jefferson City. The bluffs across the river in Callaway County sent back the sound. Surely this was a good omen!

The General Assembly greeted the portraits and the artist with applause, admiration, and enthusiasm. Soon there were shouts of "Speech . . . speech. . . ."

Smiling and happy, Bingham walked to the front of the room. He waved and bowed to friends. Then he began to speak, as he later said, "without a moment's preparation." His theme was "The Union and the Star Spangled Banner." With all the strength of his conviction he urged the preservation of the Union and lashed out at those who would secede. General applause came as he sat down, but before the day was out, it was abundantly clear that he had angered the secessionists.

Lieutenant Governor Thomas Reynolds was one who lectured Bingham on his remarks. Bingham wrote Major Rollins: "He received a good deal more than he had bargained for. . . . In fact, he is a fool, as you would say, a d—d fool." Newspapers published what Bingham insisted were "gross misrepresentations of what took place."

Summing up the day, the artist said, "I have infuriated all the traitors by boldly avowing my love for my government which they are conspiring to destroy."

The legislators then withheld judgment on the portraits, which of course meant withholding payment too, "thinking no doubt that they are punishing me." Bingham's immediate decision was to remove the Jackson and Clay portraits from the capitol. In St. Louis he thought he could put them on exhibit for a couple of weeks and make more than the thirty-five hundred dollars the state had agreed to pay him.

With Bingham, thought and action were very close together. He might have taken this "bold step," except that he was in debt to Major Rollins' bank and he felt he should ask his friend to "take stock" in his action.

As he wrote to the Major, ideas began to grow in his imagination. One of them was to take the pictures to Springfield, Illinois, where he could come in "direct and favorable contact with Lincoln." He was sure that he could sell the portraits to the state of Illinois. He proposed, also, to make public appearances. "I have become so much inspired, or excited, if you so prefer to regard it, that I can make a tolerably good Speech to accompany them, and think that they and I can draw a crowd where there are people enough to make one."

A little more than two weeks later he wrote again. The passage of time had improved things. A Resolution had been passed ordering the auditor to pay Bingham. He was to be allowed to take the portraits to St. Louis for framing and to exhibit them to the public while they were there. Strong opposition to this last provision was led in the Senate by Senator Thompson of Clay County.

What Thompson said on the floor of the Senate about the pictures rankled in Bingham's soul, as well it might. A report in part of the remarks, as printed in the Liberty (Clay County) newspaper follows:

> Why sir, this horse of Jackson is not fit to be hired out. If a livery stable man was to hire out to the Senator such a horse, he might sue him for damages and recover it. . . . We had a right to understand that the artist would make a picture of Jackson as he looked at New Orleans. Now, if my memory serves me, Jackson never had a red cloak flying about him at all. . . . the fore leg of that horse looks as if it had been lying out on the prairie for six months and the wolves had been gnawing at it. . . . I never saw a horse in good health that had not got hair on his backbone close up to the body; but this horse has not got it. Why, if the Senator from Callaway was to go to a livery stable and have such a horse offered to him, he would turn away in one grand despise.

So much for the horse Bingham had gone to such pains to paint properly!

Of the portrait of Henry Clay, Thompson had less to say. His main remark was that he had seen Clay many times but had never seen him standing "with a vermifuge almanac in his hand."

Earlier, Bingham had painted portraits of James Turner Vance Thompson and his wife. The attack by the powerful Democratic leader stung him. He wrote to Major Rollins: "Thompson of Clay made an exposition of his ignorance, stupidity, vulgarity, and malignancy which will receive its proper attention as soon as I shall be further provoked to stoop low enough to inflict punishment such as he is capable of feeling." From the rest of the letter he makes it clear that Thompson's attack was not really concerned with the pictures, but because Bingham had made the speech, "The Union and the Star Spangled Banner." As he put it to Major Rollins, ". . . when on the 8th inst. I happened to spit in the face of treason."

But once Bingham got to St. Louis with the portraits he found conditions were not good for an exhibition. Political meetings were held night and day. It was hard to rent a proper building. From Barnum's Hotel he wrote, "Everything appears to be in such a depressed condition that I cannot expect to clear much beyond the expenses of the Exhibition."

The opening was finally set for Washington's Birthday, in the small hall of the Mercantile Library Association. Bingham was suffering from a severe cold.

Into this already unhappy set of circumstances came the news that Matthias Bingham had died in Texas. As Matthias had never married, George was appointed to administer the estate which consisted mostly of several thousand acres of land near Houston. It was necessary for Bingham to go there to handle the business.

The opening on Washington's Birthday was probably canceled, and the pictures returned to Jefferson City. On February twentieth Bingham wrote Major Rollins asking for a loan of a hundred dollars to make the trip.

On March sixth he acknowledged with thanks the check from his friend. He also spoke of Lincoln's Inaugural Address. "Old Abe appears reasonable. . . . He perhaps should not have said more, and I don't think he ought to have said less. I am tired of submission to traitors. If they will force a war I am for giving them enough of it."

APRIL 12, 1861.

The firing on Ft. Sumter in South Carolina started the actual hostilities of the Civil War. The bloody agony, so long threatened, was upon the nation. It was a time of trouble everywhere, and in no place was this worse than in Missouri. There a war within a war raged. Brother fought brother; friend fought friend; wounds were opened that would be decades in healing.

Missouri never officially seceded from the Union. But thousands of Missourians, including Governor Claiborne Fox Jackson, were loyal to the cause of the South. This loyalty was particularly strong in the western side of the state where many of the settlers had come from Tennessee, Kentucky, and Virginia.

On February 18, 1861, a special Missouri state convention had been called to consider the grave matter of secession from the Union. Not one man who favored secession was elected to the convention. In his book, *Heritage of Missouri,* Duane Meyer writes, "The citizens of Missouri appear to have been overwhelmingly opposed to secession. This does not mean, of course, that they were opposed to slavery, but they did not wish to separate themselves from the Federal Union."

Bingham's devotion to the Union was so great that he considered no sacrifice too much to preserve it. Although he was fifty years old when the Civil War began, he enlisted as a private in the Irish Company of Van Horn's Battalion of the United States Volunteer Corps. By summer he had been chosen a captain in the company which belonged to the home guard.

Major Robert Van Horn had three companies of men under his command. When he took two of these out through the country, he left the guarding of Kansas City to the third company under Captain Bingham.

Bingham's company took part in one of the famous battles of the war in Missouri, the battle of Lexington. Colonel James Mulligan of Chicago was in charge of the Union forces. Opposing the Union soldiers was the Missouri state militia who had been trained and armed under the authority of Governor Claiborne Fox Jackson, a man of strong southern sympathies, who was determined to bring Missouri into the secessionist camp. The Missouri state militia was led by white-haired General Sterling Price, fondly called "Old Pap" by his men. Price was a former governor, a veteran of the Mexican War, and one of the best-known men in the state.

Mulligan had around twenty-eight hundred men from several different Union groups in his command. Price led a huge unwieldy army, many of whom were unarmed. But such was Price's appeal that as he marched toward Lexington hundreds of farmboys left the fields and joined him. Estimates of his army range from ten to twenty thousand men.

Lexington was the fifth largest city in the state and an important shipping port on the Missouri River. Bales of hemp were shipped by steamboat from there.

Mulligan and his men were first to reach Lexington. They occupied the Masonic College, which was on high ground, and began to dig earthworks for their defense. When scouts brought word that Price and his army were coming nearer, Mulligan had his men burn the bridge over Tabo Creek, five miles from Lexington. He also ordered Major Van Horn to take some men and make a stand at Machpelah Cemetery. Bingham may have been in this group that accounted for the first casualties of the battle.

Price circled the burnt bridge and laid siege to the Union soldiers. Mulligan and his men were cut off from water. The suffering of the men and horses in the blazing heat of September was almost unbearable.

Mulligan had sent word to Jefferson City, asking for reinforcements. When none came, he sent another courier by a different route, "praying for reinforcements . . . or even rations."

After three days of siege, fighting began on the eighteenth of September. The home of Oliver Anderson was used by the Union as a hospital. Three times the hospital changed hands in desperate fighting. Men knelt and fired even across the cots of the wounded. Water was so short that soldiers stole swigs from the buckets used to wash wounds. Down in the center of Lexington a cannonball lodged in a column of the courthouse. (The cannonball is still there. The Anderson house is still standing.)

On September twentieth, at one o'clock in the morning, Price's batteries began a fierce barrage against the Union position. Mulligan's men were hungry, thirsty, and worn out by the siege. The stench from the dead horses was sickening. Still, the Union soldiers felt fairly safe on the high ground. No one, not even Price and his thousands, would charge up that hill into their artillery fire.

Mulligan and his men had reckoned without knowing the Missourians.

For three days Price had been having his men gather bales of hemp from nearby Dover and Wellington, from warehouses in Lexington, from wherever they could be found. Hundreds of bales were dunked in the river and then piled in the streets.

As the light grew stronger on that cloudy morning, Mulligan saw a long dark wall along the base of the hill. It had not been there before. As he stared the wall twitched, moved forward—uphill! Behind the wall came Price's men with their deadly gunfire.

The wall was made of bales of hemp, soaking wet. In back of the hemp wall were men using levers to move the bales forward. In back of them came the soldiers. Cannon shot bounced off the soggy bales; wet hemp would not catch fire. Steadily, relentlessly, the wall moved uphill.

Twice a white flag went up without Mulligan's knowledge. He was wounded but he still would not surrender. At last he called together his officers. It was clear that reinforcements were not coming. Should they surrender to avoid needless suffering? A flag of truce was sent from the meeting. Later Mulligan said, "Many of the brave fellows shed tears. And so the place was lost."

General Price reported to Governor Jackson that he had taken many prisoners, "among whom are Colonel Mulligan . . . and 118 other commissioned officers." In materiel of war his gains were heavy. Artillery, mortars, three thousand stands of infantry arms, sabers, horses, wagons, ammunition, and "more than $100,000 worth of commissary stores."

Captain Bingham's part in the battle is unknown. Perhaps like many soldiers of many other wars he only wanted to forget about it. Price released most of his prisoners on their own parole after they promised that they would never again fight against the South.

These paroles were not often honored later; some of the soldiers were even paroled to their wives. The truth was that

Price, a generous man, simply had no way to take care of prisoners. His own men were hungry part of the time. He sent the farmboys who had joined him back to the farms, promising them that he would come again.

Bingham must have made his way back to Kansas City, about forty miles. Only a few days after the battle, Eliza gave birth to a son. The couple had been married twelve years, and a baby was a cause for much rejoicing. He was named James Rollins Bingham. So now there was a Rollins Bingham as well as Bingham Rollins!

Times were bad and money was scarce. Before the baby came, Eliza had given music lessons. She was a fine musician, and she liked to teach, but music lessons are not essentials, and her classes suffered as the war ground on.

As for Bingham, he wrote to Major Rollins, "We are all out of employment and Art is far below everything else in such times as these. I am ready to turn my attention . . . to any thing by which I can keep from sinking into debt, and secure the bare necessaries of life for those who have a right to look to me for support."

This letter went to Washington, D.C., for Major Rollins was now in Congress. He was a strong supporter of Lincoln, and they became friends. Bingham asked if a job could be found for him in Washington, however humble it might be. Even as little pay as ninety to a hundred dollars a month would help. Major Rollins undoubtedly tried, but nothing came of his efforts.

Amanda Barnes of Arrow Rock was Bingham's youngest sister. She had sons of military age, so she wrote her brother, asking his advice about their enlistment. His reply is a very long letter, only a part of which is quoted here:

"At the very commencement of the war, I was the first Missourian in the border counties to enter the service of the government as a private. I have seen much on the part of men proposing to be Unionists which I have been compelled to condemn; but the same may be said of the profession of votaries of Christianity, and does this justify us in becoming infidels? If my nephews follow my advice, those of them old enough to shoulder a musket or pull a trigger will volunteer in the service of the U.S. This is the best thing they can do for themselves and country."

Hamilton Gamble was appointed provisional governor of Missouri after Claiborne Fox Jackson left the state, although Jackson continued to insist on his right to the governorship. It was a thoroughly confused situation, especially after Jackson declared the "political ties heretofore existing between the state of Missouri and the United States of America dissolved." His "government in exile" applied for admission to the Confederacy which was granted on November 28, 1861. Gamble was a southerner who remained loyal to the Union, a moderate man, and a wise leader. Early in his term he appointed George Caleb Bingham state treasurer.

The artist was fifty-one years old and often subject to illness. Further military duty was impossible for him. But in this office he felt he could still serve Missouri and the Union. He was not particularly well trained for the task, but he agreed to take it. He went at once to Jefferson City. Eliza, Clara, Horace and the baby followed.

Eliza wrote to her sister about some of the economies the family had to make. Rollins was wearing a suit made from one of her old dresses, and Clara had fashioned a pair of boots for him from a red hood from her own cloak. Eliza was using her mother's old red woolly shawl as a wrap for the baby. The Binghams had plenty of company in "making do." All over Missouri this kind of general belt-tightening went on.

An unusual picture for Bingham, which experts place in this period, is *The Thread of Life*. Neither a genre nor a historical painting, neither a portrait nor a landscape, it is unique among Bingham's works in being an allegory.

Painted in tones of blue, pink, and ivory, it shows a woman holding a child who stands on her lap. She is draped in a classic manner. The child draws thread from a distaff behind them. The two are on a cloud bank carried through the sky by an angel. The face of the woman is much like the face of Eliza.

Rollins' birth only a short time before makes the allegory very personal.

From 1862 to 1865 Bingham toiled as state treasurer. He did not enjoy the work but he did his best. There was never any doubt cast on his absolute honesty in handling state funds. With a war swirling around him, there were chances for easy profits, but Bingham took none of them.

During his term as state treasurer, he painted two pictures that might be called "war-related." One has the lengthy title, *General Nathaniel Lyon and General Francis Preston Blair, Jr., Starting from the Arsenal Gate in St. Louis to Capture Camp Jackson.* The other is simply, *General Nathaniel Lyon, 1818–1861.*

Francis Preston Blair, Jr., was one of the men most responsible for holding Missouri in the Union. He had been an organizer of the new Republican party, a lawyer, an editor, a congressman, and a friend of Lincoln. Nathaniel Lyon was a career army officer, a West Point man, and one who had a fanatic hatred of secessionists.

At the moment Bingham pictures, they are starting into one of the most controversial situations that developed during the war in Missouri. Camp Jackson—named for Governor Jackson—had in it men who were southern sympathizers. Blair and Lyon were suspicious of their loyalty to the Union. Already Lyon had smuggled out of the state sixty thousand muskets from the Federal Arsenal in St. Louis, across the river to Illinois.

Earlier Blair had trained a sizable group of men, many of them Germans recently come to the United States, in marching and half-military demonstrations. He called them the Wide Awakes. Their choice was for the Union, and it took little to turn them into home guard.

Now Lyon heard that big guns were arriving at Camp Jackson, and he demanded that the camp surrender. Bingham showed them as they started out, Blair on a black horse, and Lyon on a white one. The men at Camp Jackson, being outnumbered by Lyon's troops and the Wide Awakes, surrendered quickly. They stacked their guns and marched from the camp as prisoners.

A crowd gathered at the gate. Many in the crowd sympathized with the prisoners. Some were for the South; some quite simply distrusted the Germans in the Wide Awakes. Shouting and name-calling began: "Damn the Dutch!" "Hurray for Jeff Davis!" Quickly the crowd turned into a mob. Rocks were thrown; pistol shots fired. In retaliation the Wide Awakes fired into the massed civilians.

The reports of the number of dead differ widely. It varies from "several civilians" to "fifteen civilians and two soldiers" to "twenty-eight dead, one a babe in arms." But there was no uncertainty in the results. Blair and Lyon had secured St. Louis for the Union. The Confederate flag that was once on the roof of the Berthold house at Fifth and Pine streets was hauled down and was not raised there again.

Blair, whom Bingham would paint again and again, went on to power and prestige in the state. Lyon was dead before the year was out in the bloody battle of Wilson's Creek. The state commissioned another single-figure portrait of Lyon after his death. It was one of those lost in the fire at the capitol.

Back and forth across the state swept the terror and devastation of the war. First one side, then the other, had the upper hand. The Civil War Centennial Commission (1961) located eleven hundred battles and skirmishes fought in Missouri boundaries. It is no wonder that war-weary Missourians said there were now five seasons of the year—"Winter, Spring, Summer, Fall, and Price's Raids."

At some undated time during Bingham's term as state treasurer, one of those raids threatened Jefferson City. Bingham became alarmed over the safety of the state money. He had been at Lexington; he did not underestimate "Old Pap." Already large sums of money had been put into St. Louis banks for safety. Convinced of the danger, Bingham loaded the remainder of the money in the treasury into a wagon and took off by night, *alone*. He drove the more than a hundred miles to St. Louis through country where any haystack might hide a guerrilla band or Confederate troops.

Price never directly attacked Jefferson City, except for a brief skirmish, late in the war. To Bingham this was unimportant. The responsibility was his, and he discharged it as he saw fit. As long as he was state treasurer, he would take care of the funds.

14

Sketch No. 21
Courtesy, St. Louis Mercantile Library

Civil War and Order No. 11

George Caleb Bingham was well acquainted with the western counties of Missouri. He had lived in Kansas City, and in Independence, both located in Jackson County. He was school director in Independence. An advertisement in the Independence *Sentinel,* July 10, 1869, reads: "Dress making by Mrs. Johnson on South Liberty Street, opposite Mr. Bingham's. Shirt making and plain sewing done to order."

Jackson County, Bates County, Cass County, and Vernon County have as their western border the Missouri-Kansas state line. Trouble there between proslavery men and abolitionists did not wait for the Civil War; it had been going on for years. In 1854 when Congress passed the Kansas-Nebraska Act, leaving the choice of slavery to the residents of those two territories, violence erupted.

Abolitionist leaders in the North, determined to bring Kansas into the Union as a free state, sent hundreds of settlers opposed to slavery to take up land. The town of Lawrence, Kansas, was largely settled by families of Free State men from New England.

Such actions outraged the Southerners. They also rushed men into Kansas to protect what they felt to be their rights. Some came from as far away as Alabama. The largest and most determined group were men from Missouri. They were called "the Border Ruffians," a name given in contempt but preserved in pride. Just before he left for Europe, Bingham considered painting a picture, *March of the "Border Ruffians,"* and asked Major Rollins for some material, but he did not carry out his plan.

Kansas held its first election November 29, 1854. Governor Andrew Reeder announced that only residents of the territory would be allowed to vote. Senator David Rice Atchison of

Missouri and other influential men in the western counties began a campaign urging Missourians to cross the state line and vote "in favor of your institutions." They were so successful in this effort that some seventeen hundred Missourians crossed over and demanded their right to vote in Kansas. The officials at the polls seem to have been afraid of violence, or else in sympathy with the out-of-staters and permitted them to cast their ballots. These fraudulent votes even made slavery legal. In the next election the proslavery men and their laws were cast out, but the Kansans did not forgive the Missourians for tampering with their elections. Both sides were armed, and clashes occurred with increasing frequency. Conditions on the Kansas-Missouri border approached anarchy.

From this unrestricted violence there came, eventually, an act of military repression visited upon the counties of western Missouri by the Union army, entitled General Order No. 11. Bingham also made that the title of his famous picture showing the cruel consequences of the order. *Order No. 11* is not Bingham's best picture, not by any standards, but it is the one by which he is best known in his home state.

By 1863 life in the western counties, which Bingham knew so well, had become so dangerous that a knock at the door in the night could mean death to the man who opened the door, and the only clue to the killers would be the sound of horses galloping away in the darkness. Stock that was safe in the barn was gone by morning. These things happened not only to proslavery men, but to those who supported the Union.

C. R. "Doc" Jennison, recently of Wisconsin but now of Kansas, was one of the leaders in the plundering expeditions. In October of 1861 he had been given a Union commission as a lieutenant colonel. His regiment, the Seventh Kansas Volunteer Cavalry, went by the nickname of "Jayhawkers."

Another nickname even more sinister to Missouri farm families was "Redlegs." Jennison's men wore red morocco leggings with their uniforms. So widespread was the looting carried out by them that for years any fine horse seen as far north as Iowa was said to be "out of Missouri by Jennison."

Because of Bingham's strong devotion to the Union, the

actions of Jennison and his Redlegs were at first a cause of concern and then of anger. Bingham warned Union leaders that Jennison's conduct was driving moderate Missourians into the Confederate army. He said that Jennison was "Price's best recruiting agent." Never one to suffer in silence, Bingham made his stand public. He appealed to men he knew in positions of influence to stop Jennison.

Major Rollins was in Congress, and Bingham sent him detailed reports on Jennison's actions. Rollins confirmed the reports and went to work on the problem. Eventually Jennison was arrested and relieved of his command. But he, too, had powerful friends who secured his release and sometime later reinstated him in the army.

Another name to be reckoned with in the Border War was that of James Henry Lane, senator from Kansas, brigadier general, and fire-eating abolitionist. He had come to Kansas from Indiana where he had been a lieutenant governor and a congressman. Jim Lane had great powers of oratory, and he could hypnotize an audience, even a hostile one. His followers called him "the Grim Chieftain," a name Missourians believed he merited after he burned the town of Osceola, Missouri, to the ground, shot nine citizens, and left with two hundred Negroes and three hundred and fifty horses and mules.

The third and most important name that must be remembered in connection with Bingham's famous painting is that of the man who gave the military order, Brigadier General Thomas A. Ewing. From a politically powerful Ohio family, Ewing had come to Kansas as a lawyer. He was a law partner of William Tecumseh Sherman, the famous Union general. Ewing was the first chief justice of the supreme court of Kansas, but he resigned in 1861 to accept a commission from Jim Lane to raise a regiment.

On the Missouri side of the border, the best known among those who led the fighting was William Clarke Quantrill.

Quantrill was a slight young man in his twenties with reddish brown hair and pale blue eyes. He, also, came from Ohio. He was a school teacher, and occasionally wrote poetry. When he came West, it was first to Kansas where he worked with abolitionists, even helping to free some slaves in Missouri. Then in a complete turnabout he became the leader of a guerrilla band of western Missourians, who fought back against their enemies with murderous ferocity.

Many of Quantrill's band were young men still in their teens. Some had been driven into resistance by the treatment their families had received from Union troops. Others were wild, reckless fellows who loved the excitement and the deadly game of war in the rolling hills. To his men Quantrill was a fantastic leader. He asked no mercy and he gave no quarter. The legend he created survives to this day.

Quantrill was not at first a part of the regular Confederate army. His men were partisans, guerrillas, "an independent band of soldiers which harasses the enemy by surprise attack." This very independence from any command other than Quantrill's made them highly dangerous fighters. They came and went at his order. President Jefferson Davis of the Confederate States was not impressed by Quantrill. It was not until 1862 that he was given a captain's commission; it did little to change the leader's operations.

Riding Charley, his big roan horse, Quantrill led his guerrillas through the timber and brush, the hills and valleys, of the western Missouri counties. The names of some who rode with him are still remembered—Frank James and his younger brother, Jesse; Cole and Jim Younger; Bloody Bill Anderson; George Todd; William Gregg. Of these men and the others, only one question was asked: "Will you follow orders, be true to your fellows, and kill those who serve and support the Union?"

Once a raid was over, Quantrill and his men rode into the countryside, out of sight. Each man in the band knew the land as well as he knew the back of his own hand. It was impossible to track them down. Family and friends sheltered them, gave them fresh horses and food. To break the power of the guerrillas, the Union command must find and destroy their hiding places.

The first move toward this end was to order the arrest of women known to be "sheltering the enemies of the Union." Seventeen women were taken to Kansas City on this charge and lodged in a rickety brick building used as a prison. The building was owned by Bingham's wife, Eliza, and it was on Grand Avenue, between Fourteenth and Fifteenth streets. Among the seventeen women were three sisters of Bloody Bill Anderson and a cousin of the Younger boys.

Ewing seems to have treated his captives with consideration. They could go out to shop under guard. They were allowed playing cards and musical instruments for pastime. But such considerations did not guarantee the safety of their prison.

In mid-morning, August 13, 1863, the timbers of the house began to buckle, the old brick walls collapsed. Horror-stricken, a crowd gathered as four dead women and thirteen others badly injured were taken from the wreckage. One of the dead was a sister of Bloody Bill Anderson; another was the cousin of the Youngers. The crowd muttered, and then raged at General Ewing.

Word of the tragedy raced like a prairie fire back to Quantrill's men, hiding in the brush. They were in no mood to consider how the dreadful accident happened. They wanted vengeance, and they wanted it *now!*

Quantrill had threatened to raid Lawrence, Kansas, stronghold of the Free Staters, before. Now was the time. There was more revenge to be had in Lawrence than anywhere else. And there was loot, too. With luck they might catch Senator Jim Lane back home from Washington in his new house. The plan was made, and the men gathered at Perdee's farm on the eighteenth and nineteenth of August.

The story of Quantrill's raid on Lawrence has been told in history, in fiction, even in motion pictures. Riding by night, the men set out. A motley band, they were joined by a group of Confederate recruits under Colonel John Holt. This brought the number up to about four hundred. The young men with Holt were raw recruits, unseasoned by gunfire, but the men with Quantrill were natural fighters, veterans of raids, skirmishes, and pitched battles.

One great superiority Quantrill and his men held was the murderous use they made of their Colt revolvers. Their skill with firearms was deadly. Each man had at least two pistols and a rifle. Quantrill on this raid had four pistols in his belt and two rifles on his saddle. They rode the best horses that could be bought—or stolen.

As they rode deeper into Kansas on the third night out, they were in unfamiliar country. They waked Kansas farmers and forced them to act as unwilling guides. Each farmer was shot as his usefulness ended. William Gregg, a Quantrill man, said that ten men were shot that night.

A little after dawn on August 21, 1863, the two thousand people of Lawrence waked to gunfire and shouting. One of the shouts was "Remember the murdered girls in Kansas City."

The order had come down from Quantrill, "Kill every man big enough to carry a gun." By nine in the morning the town was on fire, and men and boys of Lawrence were lying dead in their own yards. Women were not harmed, and some were able to save their husbands by one ruse or another. Inflamed by the liquor they had found, the guerrillas gutted the town.

Senator Jim Lane was one of the few who escaped. His new house was burned but the Grim Chieftain got away, wearing his nightshirt, and hid in a field of tall corn.

Quantrill and his men galloped out of Lawrence leaving a scene of indescribable horror. A hundred and eighty men and boys dead; eighty women left widows; two hundred and fifty children fatherless. The town on fire.

The entire nation was aroused by the savage brutal raid. It was worse than a raid: it was a massacre. Blame lay heavy on General Ewing. Quantrill had openly threatened Lawrence. Why was nothing done to stop him? Why was the town undefended?

The Eastern press thundered: "General Ewing—Where Art Thou?"

Jim Lane stormed up and down the border, demanding instant retaliation and whipping his audiences into hysteria. He went to General Ewing and helped him draw up General Order No. 11, designed to depopulate the western counties where Quantrill and his men found support. He told Ewing he would be a "dead dog" unless he not only issued the order but enforced it.

General Order No. 11 was issued from Ewing's head-quarters in Kansas City on August 25, 1863. Here it is, in part:

> All persons living in Jackson, Cass, Bates Counties, Missouri, and in that part of Vernon included in this District . . . are hereby ordered to remove from their present places of residence within fifteen days from the date thereof. . . .

Towns were excluded. It was at the farms, where Quantrill got help, that the order aimed. Hay and grain were to be taken to the nearest military station before September ninth. Any remaining fodder would be destroyed where it stood.

Doc Jennison and his Fifteenth Kansas Cavalry were among the enforcers of the order. Dr. Richard Brownlee in *Gray Ghosts of the Confederacy* says, "The revenge-seeking Jayhawkers burned all houses, food, and forage. Jennison and the cavalry robbed and murdered while performing their official duties, and their acts were so brutal that George Bingham later perpetuated their violence in his famous painting 'Order Number Eleven'. . . . In two weeks western Missouri was desolated. . . . Only six hundred persons were left in Cass County which had had a population of ten thousand before the war." He quotes a Union officer who said in writing to his wife, "It is heart sickening to see what I have seen. . . . A desolated country and men & women and children, some of them allmost naked. Some on foot and some in old wagons. Oh God."

The displaced had no place to go. They wandered. They camped out. The sick died; the weak collapsed. Some who had the means got to a steamboat landing and left, never to return. A few families got as far as Texas. The surrounding counties took in refugees, but they, too, were hard pressed.

For generations these counties were called "the Burnt District." Tall chimneys standing by fire-blackened foundations were known as "Jennison tombstones."

Down in Jefferson City Bingham heard of Order No. 11 and of the way it was being enforced. He heard of the suffering of the innocent, the wanton destruction of property. Could this be the same Union he loved and had fought for? He decided that he must do something about it himself.

He would go to General Ewing and ask that Order No. 11 be canceled.

Small but dauntless, the artist closed the door of the state treasurer's office and took the train to Kansas City. Ewing's headquarters were at the Pacific House. Bingham requested and got a hearing.

There have been many accounts of the meeting. It was a stormy one. Bingham began by making his request. Ewing refused. The order had been issued and would be carried out. Bingham recited stories of hardship visited on innocent people. Ewing was unmoved. Bingham cited his service to the Union, and his love of his country. The request he had made at first became a demand.

To Ewing, a brigadier general, the very idea that a civilian should demand what Bingham was demanding was unbelievable. There would be *no* rescinding the order.

To that flat refusal Bingham said, "If you persist in executing this order, I shall make you infamous with my pen and brush so far as I am able."

He turned on his heel and walked out of the Pacific House. His words would be associated with his painting of *Order No. 11* for all time in the Burnt District.

Bingham went back to Jefferson City, but not for one moment did he forget General Ewing, or Order No. 11. His campaign against Ewing was long and arduous; it went on for years. He did not start his painting at once. How to deal with Order No. 11 was a complicated matter. In the meantime life must go on. His family had to be considered.

In 1864, in June, the month of brides and roses, Clara Bingham was married to Thomas B. King. She was nineteen, an accomplished needlewoman who spoke both French and German. Her eye for details was so fine that her father at one time thought she should work at making steel engravings. The bridegroom was the son of Austin B. King, former governor of Missouri, and one of those who had stood with Bingham in the struggle against Jennison. After their marriage the young couple moved to Texas.

Horace Bingham was now twenty-three. He was single, and he worked with his father in the state treasurer's office. Later he worked on a farm in Cooper County.

Rollins Bingham was now three years old, a bright, appealing youngster. Bingham's letters to Major Rollins are full of his delight in this, his last child. A portrait of Rollins Bingham at about nine years, holding his schoolbooks, is as fine a portrait of a child as Bingham ever painted. The large eyes and the sensitive mouth of the boy are much like those in the portraits of his mother, Eliza.

Eliza was a loving wife, stepmother, and mother. She never wavered in her loyalty to her husband and stood by him in his convictions. During the many changes in living quarters, the journeys in which she stayed behind to do the packing and moving, and the hundred other tiresome details that came before she could "join him later," she gave no indication if her life were other than exactly as she wanted it. Eliza Bingham did not have an easy life; but she made it a good one.

Dr. Rusk, Bingham's first biographer, includes letters from Eliza to her sister telling some of the problems they faced in Jefferson City. One was the violent controversy between Bingham and B. Gratz Brown, a Liberal Republican leader and a supporter of Jennison. They almost came to blows over Jennison and his policies which Bingham abhorred. In order to attack Bingham, Eliza wrote, her husband's enemies were attacking his work as an artist. Those who opposed Bingham would see to it that he got no further commissions from the state.

Bingham's term as state treasurer ended with the end of the Civil War in 1865. He and Eliza moved back to Independence. Once there he started work on *Order No. 11*. The original title was *Martial Law,* but the picture is far better known as *Order No. 11*.

He worked in a small house near the town spring that had made Independence an important point on the early emigrant trails. The house has been spoken of as "a log cabin," but an early photograph looks much more like a rather shabby unpainted frame house.

Two paintings of *Order No. 11* were made, both about 4½ by 5½ feet. Later a smaller version was painted. The first one was done on canvas fixed onto wood panels. The unseasoned wood warped, damaging the canvas. Bingham then sewed two linen tablecloths together and painted his second picture. There are few differences between the two pictures, and those that can be detected are minor.

Order No. 11 shows a pro-Southern family being evicted from their home. Around them are Union troops—the Redlegs. From an upstairs balcony, soldiers are throwing out furniture. Wagons loaded with loot crowd the background.

In the foreground of the picture lies the body of a young man of the family who has been shot. His wife weeps over him. A gray-haired grandfather is defying a soldier who has drawn a gun. A young woman is trying to keep the old man from the soldier and a frightened little boy tugs at his grandfather's knee. A young woman prays for mercy, an older woman has fainted in the arms of a black nurse. A black man and a boy turn away from the tragic scene. In the distance rises the smoke of burning homes, and a long line of loaded wagons is being driven off toward the west.

The officer in charge sits on horseback, watching. It is generally accepted that this is General Ewing. Rollins Bingham in the Kansas City *Star,* December 5, 1909, wrote of his father's work, "In all these pictures there is but one intentional likeness of place and person and that is the likeness of Gen. Thomas Ewing in *Order No. 11.* He is the mounted officer in the middle background, facing to the left, before the plundered mansion." He also said that as a small boy he had posed for the child hanging onto his grandfather's knee.

The picture is melodramatic and stilted, but there can be no question of the moral indignation of the artist. It has been said that *Order No. 11* is not a picture, but a polemic—a controversial argument. Here for the first time in his career Bingham used his artistic talent and skill to make a strong social state-

Order No. Eleven, 1868 *Courtesy of Cincinnati Art Museum,* The Edwin and Virginia Irwin Memorial

ment. It is not his best picture, but it is certainly not a picture that any student of his work can overlook.

The paint was scarcely dry on the picture before it was famous. It was attacked and it was praised. Bingham was involved in arguments over *Order No. 11,* from 1868 when it was completed, for the rest of his life.

The attacks came in newspapers, in public meetings, and even from the pulpit. Some were because the artist, a Union man, showed Union soldiers looting and burning. Some came from those who wanted only to forget the terrible war. Some came, understandably, from those who were angry at the implied criticism of the state of Kansas.

To these last Bingham made a lengthy reply. He insisted that he put no blame on Kansas, but only on the leaders of Kansas who invoked the order, and the harsh enforcement. He wrote of some scandalous behavior of Missourians, "So you see, Sir, as honest men we have enough to make us blush at home without going abroad to find fault with our neighbors."

In fairness to General Ewing it should be said that he had his defenders. Most of the arguments rested on the military necessity for the order. Ewing's superior officer, General Schofield, insisted in 1877 that "not a life was sacrificed, nor any great discomfort inflicted in carrying out the order. . . ." Bingham's reply to this was: "Never did an equal number of words embody a greater amount of error."

The public interest in the painting indicated that steel engravings might prove popular. Bingham believed that they would sell easily. To finance the venture he borrowed five thousand dollars from Major Rollins and R. B. Price of Columbia. John Sartain of Philadelphia was to make the engraving from the "tablecloth" version. Bingham took the "wood panel" version on tour to sell subscriptions.

But he had not reckoned with the economic troubles of a country recovering from a terrible war. No other state bore more scars from the conflict than Missouri. In the Union army 13,885 died; the number of the Confederate dead was estimated at 12,000. The state was over thirteen million dollars in debt. Understandably there was little market for steel engravings, no matter what the subject.

Letters from Bingham to Rollins show the artist worrying over being unable to repay his friends. He offered to raffle off the picture, but Major Rollins would not hear of it. Finally Rollins bought Price's part of the loan, and Bingham gave him the "tablecloth picture."

The "wood panel" picture was not sold until after Bingham's death. It was then bought at auction by Colonel Joseph Wayne Mercer of Independence. Colonel Mercer, like Bingham, had served as state treasurer. The picture stayed in his home for many years. As time went on the warping of the wood became more pronounced. Eventually the Cincinnati Museum of Art in General Ewing's home state of Ohio bought it. The picture was restored to its original condition.

In 1945 the State Historical Society of Missouri acquired the "tablecloth" picture from the Rollins estate. Both versions of *Order No. 11* now hang in public galleries and may be seen in either Cincinnati or Columbia. Those who want to know Bingham should try to see the picture which absorbed so much of his later life.

Mrs. Mercer in whose home the picture hung in Independence did not like to be asked about it. To her granddaughter she would shake her head and say, "Child, it's not a happy story." It is indeed an unhappy story from a bitterly unhappy time. But from the beginning artists have mirrored their times; they do not create them. Bingham held up a mirror to the chaos and misery around him, and left it for posterity to see.

Most Bingham paintings can stand on their merits, alone. *Order No. 11* requires some knowledge of the sectional war that brought it into being.

15

Sketch No. 49
Courtesy, St. Louis Mercantile Library

Adjutant General Bingham

At the close of the Civil War, the Radical Republicans in Missouri pushed through a new state constitution. It had many harsh laws designed to punish those who had fought for the Confederate cause. One section was concerned with the "Ironclad Oath."

All preachers, teachers, lawyers, and court officers were required to swear that they had never been in armed hostility to the United States nor "ever given aid, comfort, countenance, or support to persons engaged in such hostilities." To refuse to take the oath and teach or preach or practice law without having taken it made the offender liable to a five hundred dollar fine or six months in jail or both.

In the time between the painting of the different versions of *Order No. 11,* Bingham heard of an injustice caused by the enforcement of the "Ironclad Oath" law that aroused his indignation.

Major Abner Holton Deane, a Baptist preacher in Cass County, was, like Bingham, a Union man. When war was declared, he had gone with men from his several congregations into service in the Union Army. He had been elected major and spent four years in the army. After the war he went back to his preaching.

When the new constitution was passed, he examined his conscience and decided that he could not take the required oath. (In this he had the company of many other pastors, both Roman Catholic and Protestant.) In the name of humanity he had helped women and children of Confederate families. He also, as he later wrote, "did not feel that I had received from the state my commission to preach, and the state had no right to take it from me."

Major Deane was arrested. He was taken from Cass County to Jackson County and there put into the county jail in Independence. His service in the Union army meant nothing to his persecutors.

When Bingham heard about the jailing of Major Deane, he went to visit him. The result of this was a small picture usually described as "oil on paper," 14½ inches square. The Major is seated on a straight wooden chair by a heavily barred window. An open book is on his crossed knees. On the wide stone window ledge is another book, possibly a small Bible. On the stone-slab floor is a crumpled copy of *The Baptist Journal*. There is a mattress on the floor with a woolen shawl at one end. The face of the man is calm and serene.

The whole picture is simple, unforced, and truly effective. Bingham shows clearly his wish to use his art "for the purpose of doing justice."

Many years later, when Major Deane was seventy-five, he wrote his reminiscences. A sentence in it has a most interesting insight into Bingham's way of working. "Among those who visited me was Captain Bingham, the celebrated Missouri painter. Several times he came and brought me books, and once he brought his camera and took my photograph, from which he afterward painted my portrait."

So far as can be discovered this is the first time that Bingham used the help of a camera in painting a portrait. After a good deal of research the present owners of the picture, William Jewell College at Liberty, Missouri, had the picture examined by experts at the Nelson Gallery of Art. They came to the conclusion that the picture *is* a photograph which has been retouched with oil paints. The most likely solution is that Bingham made the photograph, as Major Deane said, and colored it with oils in order to use it as a model for the larger portrait he planned. He may have gone ahead and made the portrait, which then joins the long list of those Bingham paintings not located; or he may have simply stopped with the photograph.

Whatever the solution, *Major Deane in Jail* is an artist's effort to right a wrong; it is photographed with an artist's skill.

Bingham's success in helping Major Deane was noted in

Deane's obituary in 1912. "He was released [from jail] after a short period of confinement, through the efforts of Judge Cummings, Attorney Chrissman, and George Caleb Bingham, the artist. . . ."

The constitution with the Ironclad Oath lasted ten years. The extreme position of the Radical Republicans during that time caused Bingham and many others to turn to the Democratic party. In May of 1868 Bingham was nominated a Democratic elector. Later he was prominently mentioned as a candidate for governor, but he did not campaign for the office and withdrew his name.

General Ewing, too, had made some changes. By 1870 he had returned to Ohio, and to the Democratic party. There was talk that he might be nominated for governor, or as United States senator.

Bingham heard the rumors. His old anger boiled up. In truth, it had never been very far below the boiling point. He wrote a pamphlet with the long drawn-out title of *An Address to the Public Vindicating the Work of Art Illustrative of the Federal Military Policy in Missouri During the Late Civil War.*

One sentence from the pamphlet will bear repeating for it is as true now as it was when Bingham penned it: "Constitutions and laws, however carefully framed, are no guarantee of the rights of the people when their public affairs are committed to the hands of unworthy and treacherous agents."

Ewing's political opponents appealed to Bingham for 250 engravings of *Order No. 11* to be used against Ewing in the campaign. He had to refuse them as John Sartain had not yet completed the plates.

At one time Bingham even suspected that Ewing's agents had approached Sartain, with "stronger inducements to destroy the plate than to complete it." After making a trip to Philadelphia, he decided his suspicions were unfounded. He wrote to Major Rollins about Sartain, "He seems to be a thorough gentleman, but one of those who have not the fortitude to say no to friends who continually call on him for services."

As the engravings could not be supplied in time for the

Ohio convention, Bingham had a photograph made of *Order No. 11* that could be copied. He sent that with the pamphlet he had written. The two items were widely circulated before the convention. Ewing did not receive the nomination that he sought.

In 1872 friends of Major Rollins commissioned Bingham to paint a full-length portrait of Rollins to be given to the University of Missouri. Rollins' long, devoted service had won him the title, "Pater Universitatis" (Father of the University). The slender, clean-shaven young lawyer Bingham had met in 1834 had become a dignified, commanding figure with a magnificent full beard. He was a splendid subject for a painter.

It may have been this portrait, or one of several others, that brought from critics the often repeated comment that Bingham painted best those who interested him the most. The Rollins portrait was highly successful, and it was presented at a public meeting with many speakers, much applause and acclaim.

One who spoke was Alban J. Conant, a portrait painter and professional artist. He talked about the enduring friendship between Bingham and Rollins and summed up their relationship in this way: "And next to their own kith and kin, each by the other has been the best beloved."

From his letters it seems that Bingham was not at this public meeting. He was often ill now, and this must have been the case or surely he would have been there. He wrote to Rollins about the many speeches: "They send us to immortality together."

The full-length portrait was one of those destroyed by fire, but a small study made by the artist, a bust-length portrait, still exists.

The Democratic National Convention of 1872 was held in Baltimore to nominate a president and a vice-president. Bingham went East to attend. The nominees were Horace Greeley, New York editor, and B. Gratz Brown, governor of Missouri. These nominees of the Democrats were *also* nominees of the Liberal Republicans. But nothing could stop the vote for Ulysses S. Grant, who was elected by a big majority.

Leaving Baltimore, Bingham went to New York City to

Major James S. Rollins, 1871 *Courtesy of State Historical Society of Missouri*

talk to a doctor about his health. He was plagued by coughs, colds, and indigestion. Nothing definite was learned, but he did go to Colorado for his health in the summer of 1872.

No artist can go to Colorado without painting landscapes. Bingham was no exception. He painted two. Each was a view of Pikes Peak, which he called "the heavy monarch of the mountains." In each a small, solitary figure gives perspective to the size of the majestic peak.

Also in 1872, Bingham completed a historical subject he had started sixteen years before. It was *Washington Crossing the Delaware*.

Once again the artist visited Texas to see about the land his brother, Matthias, had left and to visit his daughter Clara and her husband. He wrote to Major Rollins of Clara's children. There were five: "Boys in the majority. A promising beginning and best for a new country." (Clara Bingham King eventually had eight children.)

A long illness during 1873 kept Bingham from painting. He was sixty-two. In the fall he felt well enough to take *Order No. 11* and *Washington Crossing the Delaware* to the Industrial Exposition in Louisville. Kentucky, like Missouri, was a border state and had suffered greatly in the Civil War. Bingham thought he might find some more subscribers for engravings of *Order No. 11* there. He was disappointed.

"My picture attracts great attention in the Exposition, but as yet I realize no benefit therefrom to the Engraving." The press of the crowd bothered him; so did the noise of machinery and the "constant buzz of innumerable tongues." The managers of the art gallery at the exposition had not provided a catalogue. Bingham had printed two thousand brief descriptions of the picture, but there was no place to put them. At last all he could do was "throw them on the floor before the picture."

As 1874 came along, the artist regained his vigor. Surprisingly he took on a new job. In May Governor Woodson appointed Bingham to the board of police commissioners in Kansas City. The board then elected him president.

Gambling was rampant in Kansas City. Bingham before his appointment had made numerous complaints against "the gambling hells." Once in office he started in to eliminate them. He wrote the results to Major Rollins.

"The first evening after we were installed in power, I had, in the course of one hour, from two to three hundred gamblers turned out on the streets . . . and that without the slightest disturbance of the peace." Two weeks later he reported, "The gamblers are driven beyond our limits. The saloons are all closed on Sunday, no blood has been shed, and 'peace reigns all along the line.' "

The position on the police board paid only a small amount, three hundred dollars a year. There was still the matter of making a living for his family. So Bingham returned to painting portraits. He did, however, sound very weary when he wrote on June seventh that he was "now engaged daily in the studio, painting portraits, as the common phrase among artists 'to make the pot boil.' "

In a brief return to genre he painted a western courtroom scene, *The Puzzled Witness*. It shows a stocky witness scratching his head as if to find an answer to give the prosecutor. By his side is his faithful dog as puzzled as he is. The judge, the jury, the lawyers, are faithful to the western types Bingham had painted so often in the Election Series. But some vitality, some sureness, have gone from the artist's work. Bingham kept the painting for four years, so perhaps he, too, felt a lack in it.

Another political appointment came in 1875. Governor Hardin named Bingham Adjutant General of Missouri. His particular work was to investigate the hundreds on hundreds of war claims that had piled up after the Civil War.

Bingham plunged into the red tape. He acquired some fame for his exposure of illegal practices and dishonest claims made by those not on the muster rolls. His service in this office is the reason for the title "General" which clung to his name for many years. Eliza and Rollins stayed in Kansas City, and Bingham went alone to Jefferson City where he lived in a boarding-house.

Early in 1870 the Ku Klux Klan had begun to work in Missouri. It quickly spread its operations. Acts of terror and violence to insure white supremacy broke out. There was also horse stealing, burglary, and even murder. Governor Hardin sent Bingham to Ripley County to put a stop to Klan activities. The *Daily Tribune,* Jefferson City, reported on August 30, 1876, that he had broken up the Klan, arrested nine of the ringleaders, and brought them into court where they were convicted.

During his term as Adjutant General Bingham went to Washington to press the war claims of Missouri. The claims amounted to $180,000. He managed to get most of this allowed, but to do so, he had to spend weeks and weeks trying to see the right man at the right time. It was a tedious business.

Bingham decided that he might as well use some of the enforced leisure on his hands in painting. His first subject was Vinnie Ream, the sculptor.

She was a most unusual woman. Major Rollins had met her when he was in Congress. Eliza, too, knew of her work. Together they urged Bingham to paint her portrait. Getting Miss Ream's consent, Bingham went to her studio. He painted her in the working costume of a sculptor—a simple smock. Her lovely dark hair flows over her shoulders. Beside her he placed a clay model of her most famous work, a bust of Abraham Lincoln. She looks back toward the viewer as if she has just paused in her work, a sculptor's tool held in her right hand. It is a decorative and charming picture.

In Jefferson City this portrait painting did not go unnoticed. Bingham's political enemies jumped at the chance to criticize him. The *Missouri Statesman* said he ought to be back home, attending to business.

The answer the chivalrous Bingham made was just what could be expected. He particularly resented the use of the names of Vinnie Ream and of Florence Crittenden Coleman, granddaughter of John J. Crittenden of Kentucky, whom he also painted.

But a far more serious matter than the carping of an editor faced the artist. Eliza had been far from well the year before. He had thought she was improving, but she took a turn for the worse. Bingham returned in May to find his wife seriously ill.

It was a mental illness. Eliza was cared for tenderly, but her condition grew more grave. Bingham kept her at home for two months, but after that she had to be taken to the state mental hospital in Fulton, then named the State Lunatic Asylum. Always a deeply religious woman, Eliza believed herself to be already in heaven.

"I have the consolation that my wife suffers no pain," Bingham wrote his friend, "but seems to be gradually and peacefully traveling to the home of the blessed."

Eliza Thomas Bingham died on November 3, 1876. Bingham was desolate. The sorrowful letters he wrote Major Rollins during this sad time are still sealed. An expression of his love for Eliza, written a few months before her last illness, gives an idea of the depths of his feeling.

"A boon was conferred upon me [in her love] which I have learned by twenty-six years experience to regard as second only to my eternal salvation. I shrink from thinking what would have been my fate, and that of my motherless children, if this rare and excellent woman so precisely adapted to my wants and allways adapting herself to my eccentricities, had not been given to me . . . my love has been so watered by her goodness, that it has increased tenfold since we were wed."

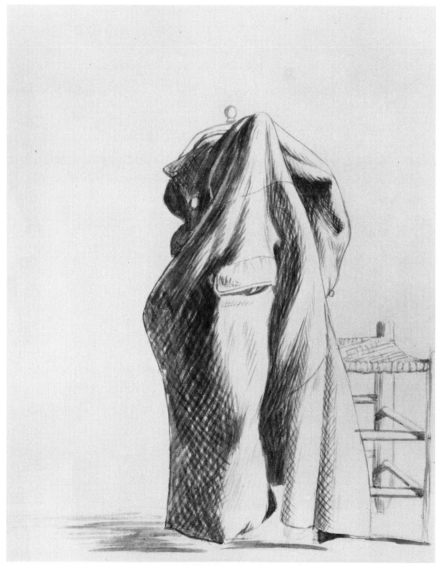

16

Sketch No. 112
Courtesy, St. Louis Mercantile Library

A Man to Remember

Spiritualism was much discussed and practiced at this time in the United States. After Eliza's death Bingham was caught up in the movement. Once he was sure that he had seen and talked to his dead wife, and that she had kissed him. An unfinished picture, found in his studio after his death, has the title, *The Pleague of Darkness*. Bingham historians think this picture may have been an outgrowth of his interest in spiritualism.

During his loss and unhappiness, Bingham was fortunate to have friends to whom he could turn. Work was his best solace, always. For several weeks in the summer of 1877 he stayed at Forest Hill, home of the Nelson family, in Boonville.

The Nelson house is the subject of one of Bingham's attractive small landscapes. In front of the tall-columned house stands a covered carriage. It belongs to the doctor who has come to care for the Nelson's daughter, Mrs. Birch, at the birth of her son. A dog is barking to announce the doctor's arrival. In the foreground is a nurse with three of the younger Birch children —one of whom was named George Bingham Birch.

The finest picture painted during this period in Bingham's life—and possibly the best of all his single figures—was started that summer at Forest Hill. The picture, called *The Palm Leaf Shade,* is not so much a portrait as an impressionistic study.

Margaret Nelson Birch, a lovely young woman with sparkling dark eyes and enchanting dimples, is seated in a summer garden. She shades her eyes from the force of the sun with a palm-leaf fan. The shadow of the fan falls across her face with the full light above and below. There is a luminous quality about the whole scene, so that the light seems to come *from* the picture. It is the light filling the canvas that is the special glory of *The Palm Leaf Shade.*

By 1878 the Impressionist movement in France was gathering strength. Monet, Pissarro, Renoir, and others were experimenting with color to show what the eye really sees. The airy light playing over surfaces of their pictures, their use of warm

The Palm Leaf Shade, 1878 *Courtesy of Nelson Gallery—Atkins Museum, Kansas City, Missouri* (Nelson Fund)

and cool colors, were part of their new techniques. *En plein air* is the French term used to describe painting light outdoors, rather than in the studio.

Bingham, half a world away from Paris, on a high bluff above the Missouri River, made the discovery on his own. With no tutoring he painted Margaret Nelson Birch in her mother's sunlit garden *en plein air*. When the picture was finished she was far more than a pretty young woman wearing a white hat with a pink feather—she was the reality of summer.

An International Exposition was opening in Paris in April 1877. Bingham had high hopes of being named a delegate from the United States. He went to Washington to try to advance his cause, but nothing came of his efforts.

The Palm Leaf Shade, which he had started in Boonville, was completed in Washington. He also worked while he was there on a picture that Major Rollins wanted of his granddaughter, Eulalie Rollins Hockaday.

Eulalie was to be painted as *Little Red Riding Hood.* It was a favorite subject of the period. Bingham sketched his idea —a little country girl with a tattered dress, droopy stockings, and her hair tangled in curls. Eulalie's mother was so upset, that Bingham patiently reworked his whole plan.

Instead, Eulalie was dressed in a pretty blue dress with a scarlet hood. Her curls were brushed and neatly arranged. In place of Bingham's tin pail, she carried a basket covered with a linen napkin. The background is a conventional "forest" with a rather uninterested wolf peering around a tree trunk. If the mother had allowed the artist to have his way, it might have been a much better picture.

The cough that had troubled Bingham for so long kept hanging on. His general health was not good. In St. Louis he consulted a doctor who used "magnetic treatments." For a time these helped, and he urged Major Rollins to try them, too.

The old controversy with Ewing was revived in 1877. Once again Bingham went into print with a scathing attack on the Ohioan. Ewing was forty-eight, and at the height of his powers. Bingham was sixty-five and plagued with illness. In the coming

Ohio Democratic state convention Ewing was nominated for Congress, and in November he was elected. It appeared that he had finally won over his old opponent.

Bingham's work as Adjutant General was finished in 1877. He thought of retiring from public life and was looking forward to spending all his time painting. However, a new opportunity came his way and he could not turn it down.

"The Hon. G. C. Bingham has entered upon his duties at the State University as Professor of the School of Art." The announcement was in the Boonville *Weekly Eagle,* October 12, 1877.

No school of art had existed in the University of Missouri up to this time. Bingham was the first man to hold the professorship. The work was not demanding. It consisted largely of an annual lecture on the subject of art, to be open to the public. A studio for his use was set up in the Normal Building in Columbia.

At his own suggestion Bingham went to St. Louis to select plaster casts from the antique for the studio. He sent to Kansas City for his paintings to be placed on the walls. Originally the position carried no salary, but the professor was allowed to take students for private instruction, if he wished. He taught some classes at Stephens College, also in Columbia.

To one of his students, Miss Amanda Austin, he made a gift of a picture of two small spaniel dogs, lying on the brim of a beaver hat. The title is *Guarding the Master's Hat.* It is a copy of a similar picture by Sir Edwin Landseer.

On January 3, 1878, Bingham wrote to Major Rollins about "My more than friend, Mrs. M. A. Lykins. You may allude to the fact of our matrimonial engagement in such terms as you think proper."

The grief of the artist at losing Eliza was deep and sincere, but as one of his kinswomen said, Bingham was not a man to be content without a wife. He had known Mrs. Lykins for a long time. She was the widow of Dr. Johnston Lykins, prominent Kansas Citian, who had died two years before. Mrs. Lykins and Eliza Bingham had worked together "in behalf of the orphans' home of Kansas City."

Self-Portrait, 1877 Lent by the Kansas City, Missouri, Public Library *Courtesy of Nelson Gallery—Atkins Museum, Kansas City, Missouri* (Nelson Fund)

At the time of the "matrimonial engagement," Mrs. Lykins was in charge of the Lykins Institute, a home for the widows and orphans of Confederate veterans. Her maiden name was Martha (Mattie) Livingston.

A self-portrait Bingham painted in 1877 may have been made as an engagement gift. It shows a man who looks a bit younger than sixty-six. A photograph taken two years later reveals the ravages of the years much more clearly. Still, a man should have the privilege of painting himself as he sees himself—and that was what Bingham did. The portrait is made with the artist holding his drawing board. He looks across it at his viewers. A hidden smile in the eyes makes it easy to overlook the weariness in the lines of his face. It is a portrait that appeals to the heart.

With the spring of 1878 Bingham went to Texas. He enjoyed these Texas trips. If he ever made any paintings there, they have not come to light. Perhaps he liked a vacation from art now and then. Clara had six children for him to play with and make sketches for as he had for the Rollins children. The reason for this particular trip was undoubtedly that he wanted to tell, not write, Clara of his plan to remarry.

The wedding took place on June 19, 1878. A lengthy, highly ornamented account was carried in the Kansas City *Times*. The ceremony was held at eight o'clock in the morning at the Lykins Institute. Some quotations from the newspaper follow:

> The parlors in which the interesting ceremonies that were to unite culture and taste, to artistic honors and ability . . . were festooned with fragrant flowers . . . from the centre of the ceiling of the back parlor, under which stood the high contracting parties, was a magnificent wedding bell, fully three feet across . . . constructed of the sombre bloom of the smoke tree, ornamented with heliotrope and honeysuckle. . . .
>
> As the pair stood there, he the successful artist whose well-wielded brush has painted pictures that shall live forever, and she the acknowledged equal in taste, aesthetic culture, and executive ability, the scene was not joyous but impressive.
>
> The congratulations were prompt and hearty, all the friends but one being younger than the newly married couple. At 9 o'clock a most bountiful breakfast was partaken of by the assembled guests—a royal feast—its real and true description would be impossible.
>
> At 10 o'clock the General and his wife . . . were driven to the depot and took the cars to Denver for a few weeks.

During the time they were in Colorado, Bingham made sketches of the mountains. One he completed and exchanged for 160 acres of land in Linn County, "near the Hannibal and St. Joe. Rail Road."

Early in November Bingham was appointed commissioner from Missouri to help select a design for a monument to General Robert E. Lee. The first meeting was to be in Richmond, Virginia. He wrote Major Rollins, asking for two passes on the Baltimore and Ohio Railroad so that he could take Mrs. Bingham with him. In December they returned to Columbia.

A little story of Bingham and his third wife during one stay in Columbia has been told and retold. Perhaps it took place on this December visit. They had rooms at Stephens College and at their first meal there the waitress, in passing a dish of food, caught her sleeve in Bingham's wig. Off it came, and it was carried halfway down the table. Great was the embarrassment of the dinner guests, but Bingham took it philosophically. "As I was not able to keep my own hair on my head, how should I hope to keep anyone else's?"

The couple's time was divided between Columbia and Kansas City. While in the latter place they lived at the Lykins Institute. His wife's ability in management impressed the artist. "She overlooks every foot of the place and allows no idle hands upon it," he wrote Major Rollins. "I think I can safely say in the highest sense of the term, she is no ordinary woman."

A severe attack of pneumonia in the winter of 1879 kept Bingham abed for weeks. The annual public art lecture at the university was set in March, but he was too ill to deliver it. He wrote out the speech and Major Rollins gave it in his place. The title was *"Art, the Ideal of Art, and the Utility of Art."* As this was the only formal expression Bingham made of his theories on the subject to which he devoted his whole adult life, it deserves careful attention.

The lecture was divided into three parts that correspond to the three divisions in the title. The first, "Art," was a general statement of his major ideas. He stated, "Michael Angelo whose sublime and unrivalled productions, both in painting and sculpture, certainly entitle him to be regarded as good authority in all that related to Art, clearly and unhesitatingly designates it [Art] as 'The imitation of nature.' "

This, too, was Bingham's belief. He told a story from the Greek about two rival painters who entered into a contest. One painted a picture of grapes so perfect that birds flocked to eat them. The other painted only a curtain, but it was so well done that his rival reached out his hand to move the curtain and see the picture he supposed was behind it. "Such adherence to . . . the truth of nature, constitutes what would properly be called the truth of Art. . . ."

The painter "must study nature in all her varied phases. . . . He may consider every theory . . . but he must trust his own eyes and never surrender the deliberate and matured conclusions of his own judgment to any authority however high."

The second part, "The Ideal of Art," has a particular sentence that applies to Bingham's own work: "Artists permit themselves to be absorbed only by what they love. . . . the ideal in Art is but the impressions made upon the mind of the artist by beautiful or Art subjects in external nature . . . Art power is the ability to receive and retain these impressions so clearly and distinctly as to be able to duplicate them upon our canvass."

In relation to his many portraits the following observations are especially interesting. Bingham says that many people "who have obtained their ideas of Art from books" think that a painter should "impart to his work the *soul* of his sitter." With this view he is in complete disagreement. He could not do so, if "my life and even my eternal salvation depended on such an achievement. . . ." Instead, "There are lines to be seen on every man's face which indicate to a certain extent the nature of the spirit within him . . . they reveal the thoughts, emotions, and to some extent the mental and moral character of the man. The clear perception and practiced eye of the artist will not fail to detect these; and by tracing similar lines upon the portrait he gives it the expression which belongs to the face of his sitter. . . . he has done all that Art can do."

The last section, "The Utility of Art," is shorter than the other two. The reader can sense the weariness of the painter as he struggled to put down his thoughts. For a man of action such a task is difficult in the best of times and Bingham was no longer vigorous. His central paragraph has this concluding sentence: "As the growth, strength and development of the body depend on food demanded by its natural appetites, so must the growth and development of the soul, and its capacity for enjoyment, depend upon the spiritual food demanded by those tastes peculiar to and a part of its nature."

And then the last. Always the thought of his country, the Union, the Republic. "And this glorious Republic of ours, stretching its liberal sway over a vast continent, will perhaps be best known in the distant ages of the future by the imperishable monuments of Art which we may have the taste and genius to erect."

Early in May, feeling stronger, Bingham went to Columbia and stayed with Major Rollins. It was the fifth of July when he went back to Kansas City. Perhaps he had lingered a little extra time to celebrate the Fourth of July at La Grange. It would be a special time for these two men who cared so much about their country, and who had lived to see so much happen to it. Now the flags had been put up for next year; the rolling oratory was stilled. The band had stopped playing and wrapped its instruments against the humid Missouri heat. The last freezer of home-made ice cream was emptied. The night was warm and only an occasional Roman candle glittered in the sky. There was time to sit and think, to remember.

July is hot in Missouri, "growing weather," when the corn grows all night. On the morning of the fifth, C. B. Rollins remembered, he was asked to get out a carriage and team and drive his father and his father's friend to the depot. With the weather what it was he would have started early and driven the high-stepping bays at a leisurely pace so as not to lather them up.

The few miles from La Grange to Columbia allowed a look at the crops on either side of the road. A good year for farmers. Both lawyer and artist understood the importance of crops for Missouri, and knew how to tell a fertile field from "hard-scrabble."

The depot was a branch line of the Wabash, St. Louis & Pacific. It was the old North Missouri railroad that had been taken over by the Wabash only that year—1879. To get to Kansas City, Bingham would have to change at Centralia.

As they waited for the train, Bingham and Rollins stood talking on the platform. Weeks together, and still there was much to say. Young Rollins lifted out Bingham's luggage and the portfolio that was never far from the artist's hand. He might have listened to the talk. Was it about the new long-distance telephone from Jackson to Cape Giradeau? Was it about the new School of Engineering for the University of Missouri? Or did the talk start with "Remember . . . remember when . . . ?" Perhaps, instead, they were talking about the new portrait Bingham had begun of his namesake, George Bingham Rollins.

Puffing and snorting, the train groaned to a stop at the station. Young Rollins carried on the luggage and saw his father's friend settled on the green plush seat. The windows were open, of course, and Bingham may have leaned out and taken his old friend's hand in good-bye. The tall imposing lawyer with his handsome full beard smiled up at the small-statured artist above him.

"Good-bye . . . Come back soon . . . Take care . . . Good-bye. . . ."

The whistle on the Wabash engine hooted, and Major Rollins stepped back. Bingham took a last look and wave, and then sat back for the little journey to Centralia. Out the window he saw the red brick buildings of Christian College and smiled at the pretty young ladies on the summer-green campus.

The train gathered speed and click-clacked through the country around Columbia. As he looked out the window Bingham may have remembered many things. Miss S. and her aristocratic family, Elizabeth with her black satin hair and cameo face, Eliza—he had met her at his studio on Guitar Street. Or he may have been thinking ahead to Mattie and the Lykins Institute. There was a portrait he had started before he became ill—Judge Waldo's child. He must finish that and deliver it.

And there was always Thomas Ewing. Bingham had been deeply disturbed by a rumor from Ohio that Ewing might be presidential or vice-presidential material in the election of 1880. When he came down with pneumonia, the doctor had insisted that he forget his old feud. Then in June the news arrived that Ewing was running for governor of Ohio. B. Gratz Brown of Missouri with whom Bingham had been both friend and enemy, had come out in favor of Ewing. Unable to keep quiet, Bingham had written to the press in reply, and Brown had replied to *him*. During his stay in Columbia, Bingham had written a long carefully drafted article on Ewing and Order No. 11. It was in his portfolio.

But the coach was warm and he was still weak from his illness. The old warrior deliberately put from his mind thoughts of Ewing, or Brown, or Senator George Vest who had entered the fray. He would think of other things. There was the exhibit of his work last spring in the English and Art building at the university. Many men and women came. As he talked with them, he had explained that he wanted to paint more Missouri pictures . . . Camp Meeting in Missouri . . . A County Fair in Missouri . . . A Circus Day in Missouri. The idea nudged him. He leaned back and closed his eyes. It would take work, planning, but he would do it. He would start as soon as. . . . So much to do . . . so much to do. . . .

"Cen—tray—lyuh! Cen—tray—lyuh!"

Bingham started up from his daydream. He gathered up his luggage. It would be good to get back home. He hoped the Kansas City train would be on time.

George Caleb Bingham died on July 7, 1879, at the Lykins Institute in Kansas City.

He was feeling unwell when he got off the train and on the next day, Sunday, his temperature began to rise. At nine in the evening a doctor was called. He spent the night at Bingham's bedside. Once Bingham roused and spoke to the doctor to say that he was preparing an answer to B. Gratz Brown's last attack and that he would finish it "as soon as he was well." His temperature continued to rise and could not be broken.

By Monday morning Bingham was in a coma. He died at eleven thirty. His death came from a disease then called cholera morbus. This is not the Asiatic cholera which came in epidemics upon the country, but what is known in current times as gastro-enteritis. It is possible that the bouts of "stomach trouble" and "dyspepsia" from which Bingham had suffered so long were less acute forms of the same illness. He was sixty-eight years old.

The July heat was worse now. "It was too hot to go out at all," an Independence newspaper said on the day of his death. A decision was reached to have the burial on Wednesday morning at ten o'clock at the home, "a mile and a half south of the city limits" on the Westport Road.

The funeral was an outpouring of public honor. Many, many people came. The minister was Dr. Chambliss of the Calvary Baptist Church who had married Bingham to Mrs. Lykins thirteen months before. After some music and Dr. Chambliss' sermon, Dr. Laws, president of the University of Missouri, spoke. Then Major James Sidney Rollins gave the eulogy.

Every newspaper in the area carried an account of the services, and each one spoke of the beauty of Major Rollins' words. It is sad that no reporter took them down. Their great power and their loving tribute to the memory of a friend was mentioned over and over. As one anonymous writer said, "Those who heard it will always carry with them a memory. . . . It made us think better of human nature, and teaches us that after all, men are better than we think."

Bingham was buried in Union Cemetery, near the south edge of the city. He was carried to his grave by eight pallbearers, among them his old commanding officer in the Union Army, Colonel Van Horn.

In the state where he had lived most of his life, Bingham was sincerely mourned. Even those who disagreed with him, and there were many, recognized his fearless following of his own conscience and respected him. The *Kansas City Mail,* July 7, 1879, said, "No man was better known in Missouri, either as an artist or a powerful writer, or a patriot of incorruptible integrity."

An editorial in the *Kansas City Journal* read, "As a citizen General Bingham was a noted man, always . . . society has lost a man who, whatever his connection with public affairs, has left behind him that noblest of all characteristics—that of an honest man."

A few days after his father's death, Rollins Bingham, then eighteen, took the article from his father's portfolio that had been prepared as an answer to B. Gratz Brown to the *Kansas City Journal.* It was published July 25, 1879.

The article was a long one, covering an entire page. Brown had been defending Ewing on his issuance of Order No. 11. Bingham replied: "You inform the public that you do not intend to follow me down into the mire of defamation. It is true, sir, you do not follow me in that direction, but you go down alone, leaving me above. Defamation consists of falsehood of the most reprehensible kind, and until you shall be able to show that I have given utterance to a malicious untruth either in regard to yourself or your record, which I here challenge you to do, all impartial persons will believe that the grave accusations which you thus direct against me can be hurled with far greater truth against yourself."

From this disclaimer of dishonesty, which rankled deep, Bingham began to give proof after proof of the "infamies of Order No. 11." One of these was the testimony of Union General Richard C. Vaughan of Lexington, "a gentleman of high standing, culture, and unimpeachable veracity whom you know well and who was (not like yourself, a thousand miles off) an eyewitness of the horrors attending the enforcement of this infamous edict . . . General Vaughan fully indorsed my charges against General Ewing as true in every particular.

"The torch was freely used, and dense columns of smoke from burning dwellings were seen far and wide over the scourged district and men were ruthlessly shot down in the very act of obeying the order.

"All this you saw portrayed in my picture. . . . All this, too, was fully known to Gen. Ewing. Reports reached him continually in regard to what was taking place; and though he had an ample force at his command he did not issue an order or lift a hand to prevent it. On the contrary, those most prominent in this diabolical work of robbery, devastation and murder had free access to his headquarters, and no crime which they saw proper to commit received a rebuke, much less punishment from him."

Bingham then wrote of "a poor innocent citizen named Rout," who was arrested and cast into military prison and was found next morning in the Missouri River with a rope or chain around his neck. Another man, Crenshaw, was put into the same prison and threatened with murder unless he signed over his property, "a large lot of mules amounting to thousands of dollars." Bingham said that these are facts "which are notorious in Kansas City and with which all the inhabitants living there are perfectly familiar."

Ewing had also, Bingham said, suppressed Democratic newspapers in the district as at that time he believed all Democrats to be "rebels and rebel sympathizers." Those papers named were the *Caucasian,* the *Chicago Times,* the *Crisis,* the *Cincinnati Enquirer* and the *New York World.*

In concluding Bingham put into print letters from prominent men supporting his view. Union General Odon Guitar wrote that "the measure in question . . . was unnecessary, unwise, cowardly, and barbarous." Former Governor Willard Hall wrote that he had asked General Schofield to have the order revoked.

Five closely packed columns in the *Kansas City Journal* carried the story. It was also in the *St. Louis Post Dispatch* and in many other newspapers in both Missouri and Ohio. "A Voice from the Tomb" was one of the headlines used.

The campaign in Ohio between Ewing and Foster for governor was turned into a heated one. Still, it seemed reasonable that Ewing would win. He had much on his side.

When the election at last arrived, Ewing lost to Foster—by less than 3 percent of the votes. The long battle was over.

Ewing never again tried for high political office. He later moved to New York City and practiced law there.

Some years after Bingham's death, C. B. Rollins was in New York City and called on Ewing. The talk turned to Missouri, the war, and inevitably to Bingham. Rollins asked how Ewing felt about the artist, after all these years. The answer he received shows a good deal about the character of both men.

Ewing said that he held no resentment toward Bingham.

Then, hesitating a moment, he said that Bingham was "a man of the highest ideals, but with so little understanding of the necessities of war that before he would commandeer a mule or a load of hay from a farmer in the line of march he would first have to consult the constitution to see that he was within the law."

These last few pages of this book, which concern Bingham's death and its effect, have dealt mostly with his accomplishments as a public man. Little was said at that time about his work as an artist. Now, nearly a hundred years later, the *artist* is the man most recalled. Time has given to Bingham a place in American art that is peculiarly his own—that of a man untrained in any special school of art, who loved his frontier world and painted it.

His paintings have the *integrity* of the man, so often mentioned in the columns written after his death. They are honest, unsentimental, objective. Bingham did not intrude himself on his work (except in *Order No. 11*). He was self-taught, and he never stopped working and learning.

As a portrait painter, he began and ended his life. Some of his portraits are brilliant. He did not flatter, he did not caricature. Where life had left lines, thinned curls, thickened the jawline, added a mole or subtracted a dimple, Bingham painted what he saw. In this, as he said in his lecture on art, "if he [the artist] gives them correctly, he has done all that Art can do."

As a draftsman, Bingham was superb. The sketches that he created as "source material" for his multifigured paintings could stand alone as an accomplishment for any artist. There is authority in them; they are done with quick, sure strokes by a man who knew what he was doing and how to do it.

The world of the frontier that he showed in his genre paintings is gone now. It is further away today than the moon or Mars. But like those heavenly bodies, it has an influence on our times. For how can we understand our present unless we know our past? Bingham recorded it on canvas—the western expansion, the brawling rivermen, the eager politicians, the fur trappers, and always the powerful, unknowable rivers. In his genre paintings especially, as John Francis McDermott has said of them, "A lost world lives forever. This is the magic of painting."

Considerable fame came to Bingham in his lifetime. There was enthusiasm for his work in his home state, which must have given "the Missouri artist" genuine satisfaction.

But he had his critics, too. An eastern critic said of *The Jolly Flatboatmen*, "It was a vulgar subject, treated vulgarly." Similar things were said about *Raftmen Playing Cards*. This was not high art, as eastern critics understood the term. It was only people behaving like people.

People still know and love Bingham's work. A blank map of the United States marked with the places where Bingham paintings are located will show that they extend from Maine to California, from Wisconsin to Louisiana. No longer can George Caleb Bingham be only regarded as "the Missouri artist"; he is, as Major Rollins prophesied long ago, *an American artist*.

An unknown staff writer for the *Bulletin* of the American Art-Union wrote after a visit Bingham made to New York: "All these works are thoroughly American in their subjects, and could never have been painted by one who was not perfectly familiar with the scenes they represent. It was this striking nationality of character, combined with considerable power in form and expression which first interested the Art-Union in these productions, notwithstanding the existence of obvious faults. . . . His figures have a vitality about them. They look out of their eyes. They stand upon their legs. They are shrewd or merry or grave or quizzical. They are not mere ghosts—mere pictures of jackets or trowsers with masks attached to them. . . ."

So it was when this comment was written in 1849. So it is today. George Caleb Bingham painted men, women, and children, and *brought them to life*.

Selected Bibliography

Bloch, E. Maurice. *George Caleb Bingham; A Catalogue Raisonné.* Berkeley and Los Angeles, University of California Press, 1967.

Bloch, E. Maurice. *George Caleb Bingham: The Evolution of an Artist.* Berkeley and Los Angeles, University of California Press, 1967.

Brownlee, Richard S. *Gray Ghosts of the Confederacy: Guerilla Warfare in the West, 1861–1865.* Baton Rouge, Louisiana State University Press, 1958.

Christ-Janer, Albert. *George Caleb Bingham of Missouri: The Story of an Artist.* New York, Dodd, Mead & Co., 1940.

Cowdrey, Mary Bartlett. *The American Academy of Fine Arts and the American Art-Union.* 2 vols. New York, New-York Historical Society, 1953.

Davis, W. B. and Durie, D. S. *An Illustrated History of Missouri.* St. Louis, Mo., A. J. Hall; Cincinnati, R. Clark, 1876.

Flexner, James Thomas. *First Flowers of Our Wilderness, American Painting.* Boston, Houghton Mifflin, 1947.

Freedgood, Lillian. *An Enduring Image: American Painting from 1665.* New York. Thomas Y. Crowell Company, 1970.

Hawes, Charles C. *This Place Called Kansas.* Norman, Okla., University of Oklahoma Press, 1952.

Larkin, Lew. *Bingham: Fighting Artist,* Kansas City, Mo., Burton, 1954.

McDermott, John Francis. *George Caleb Bingham: River Portraitist.* Norman, Okla., University of Oklahoma Press, 1959.

Meyer, Duane. *Heritage of Missouri.* Rev. ed., St. Louis, State Publishing Co., 1965.

Mering, John Vollmer. *The Whig Party in Missouri.* Columbia, Mo., University of Missouri Press, 1967.

Morrison, Wm. M. *Morrison's Stranger's Guide to the City of Washington and Its Vicinity,* 2nd edition, Washington City, 1844.

Reavis, L. U. *St. Louis the Future Great City of the World: Centennial Edition.* St. Louis, Mo., Barnes, 1876.

Rusk, Fern Helen. *George Caleb Bingham: The Missouri Artist.* Jefferson City, Mo., Stephens Publishing Co., 1917.

Smith, W. B. *James Sidney Rollins.* New York, De Vinne Press, 1891.

Vestal, Stanley. *The Missouri.* Bison Book edition, Lincoln, University of Nebraska Press, 1964.

Public Places Where Bingham Paintings May Be Seen

(Note: Every effort has been made to make this list accurate, but art galleries often change their displays, or pictures may be on loan to other galleries. If you do not find Bingham pictures displayed, ask at the museum desk for information. The list is alphabetical by cities.)

Arrow Rock, Missouri: The Tavern

Boonville, Missouri: Boonslick Regional Library (Main Street)

Boston, Massachusetts: Museum of Fine Arts

Cambridge, Massachusetts: Peabody Museum, Harvard University

Cincinnati, Ohio: Cincinnati Art Museum

Columbia, Missouri: State Historical Society of Missouri. Also portraits in the University of Missouri (Columbia)

Detroit, Michigan: Detroit Institute of Arts

Fort Worth, Texas: Kimbell Art Museum

Hartford, Connecticut: Wadsworth Atheneum

Independence, Missouri: Jackson County Historical Society (Old Jail Museum)

Kansas City, Missouri: William Rockhill Nelson Gallery of Art

Liberty, Missouri: William Jewell College

Los Angeles, California: Los Angeles County Museum of Art

Madison, Wisconsin: State Historical Society of Wisconsin

Newark, New Jersey: Newark Museum

New Orleans, Louisiana: New Orleans Museum of Art (Not on display at this time)

New York, New York: Metropolitan Museum of Art and the Brooklyn Museum

Port Gibson, Mississippi: Chamberlin-Hunt Academy

St. Louis, Missouri: City Art Museum and Missouri Historical Society (both in Forest Park), Boatmen's National Bank of St. Louis and St. Louis Mercantile Library (both downtown), Washington University, Sternberg Hall

San Diego, California: The Fine Arts Society of San Diego
Tulsa, Oklahoma: Thomas Gilcrease Institute of American History and Art
Washington, D.C.: Corcoran Gallery of Art

Index

(Page numbers in italics indicate illustrations.)

About the Author

Alberta Wilson Constant is well known to young people for her popular and highly acclaimed novels, all of which have a richly authentic turn-of-the-century American background: *Miss Charity Comes to Stay,* ,*Those Miller Girls, The Motoring Millers,* and *Willie and the Wildcat Well.*

Mrs. Constant was born in Texas but spent her school years in Oklahoma and was graduated from Oklahoma State University. She was encouraged by several of her professors to write, and later she took classes in professional writing at the University of Oklahoma.

She became interested in George Caleb Bingham, "the Missouri artist," after moving with her husband and two children to Independence, Missouri, in 1946. First, she heard of the Civil War controversy surrounding a military order known as "Order No. 11" and of Bingham, the courageous artist who painted a picture of the destruction wreaked by that order. Delving more and more into local history, she discovered other paintings by Bingham, who had once lived in Independence. Soon she was traveling elsewhere to see his art. Out of her deep interest, she decided to write his biography—and also a story of his times.

About her work, Mrs. Constant writes: "My research carried me many miles, to many people. . . . Each time I saw a new piece of Bingham's work, I went back to my desk all the more determined to tell his story for young people. It seems to me now, as it did when I set out five years ago, that his is an American triumph."